CONTEMPORARY AMERICAN LITERATURE

(1945–PRESENT)

Jerry Phillips, Ph.D.
General Editor

Department of English
University of Connecticut, Storrs

Michael Anesko, Ph.D.
Adviser and Contributor

Director, Honors Program in English
Pennsylvania State University

Erik V. R. Rangno
Principal Author

Facts On File
An imprint of Infobase Publishing

Contemporary American Literature (1945–Present)

Facts On File, Inc.
An imprint of Infobase Publishing
132 West 31st Street
New York NY 10001

ISBN-10: 0-8160-5671-4
ISBN-13: 978-0-8160-5671-2

Library of Congress Cataloging-in-Publication Data
Rangno, Erik V. R.
   Contemporary American literature : 1945-present / Erik V.R. Rangno.
     p. cm.— (Backgrounds to American literature)
   Includes bibliographical references and index.

   ISBN 0-8160-5671-4 (alk. paper)

  1. American literature—20th century—History and criticism.
2.Postmodernism (Literature)—United States. I. Title. II. Series.
PS225.R36 2005
810.9'0054—dc22   2005020830

Facts On File books are available at special discounts when purchased in bulk quantities for businesses, associations, institutions, or sales promotions. Please call our Special Sales Department in New York at (212) 967- 8800 or (800) 322-8755.

You can find Facts On File on the World Wide Web at http://factsonfile.com

Printed in the United States of America

VB PKG 10 9 8 7 6 5 4 3 2

This book is printed on acid-free paper.

Acknowledgments
p. 7: U.S. Navy photo by Chief Warrant Officer Seth Rossman
pp. 14, 23, 25, 37, 41: Library of Congress, Prints and Photographs Division
p. 45: © Warren J. Plath, Mortimer Rare Book Room, Smith College
p. 49: Courtesy Library of Congress
p. 65: © Rubén Guzmán
p. 75: www.availablelightphoto.com

DEVELOPED AND PRODUCED BY DWJ BOOKS LLC

CONTENTS

PREFACE

The five volumes of *Backgrounds to American Literature* explore 500 years of American literature by looking at the times during which the literature developed. Through a period's historical antecedents and characteristics—political, cultural, religious, economic, and social— each chapter covers a specific period, theme, or genre.

In addition to these six chapters, readers will find a useful time-line of drama and theatrical history, poetry and prose, and history; a glossary of terms (also identified by small capital letters throughout the text); a biographical glossary; suggestions for further reading; and an index. By helping readers explore literature in the context of human history, the editors hope to encourage readers to further explore the literary world.

1. AMERICAN LITERATURE SINCE 1945

Because it is so diverse in theme and style, and because critics and historians of literature do not yet have sufficient perspective to make enduring judgments, American literature since the end of World War II is difficult to categorize. Still, there are some clear trends and influences that can be identified, and it is certain that contemporary American literature refelcts the complexity, the unrest, and the multi-culturalism of contemporary American society.

War

Both World War II and the Vietnam War left distinctive marks on American literature. After World War II, returning soldiers were not dis-illusioned to the degree that veterans of World War I had been, perhaps because the world had grown used to carnage on a grand scale and perhaps because the cause for which nations fought World War II seemed nobler. Yet a good deal of the fiction that emerged from the war portrays a sense of human helplessness in the face of the de-structive forces unleashed on the world by advanced military technology, including the nuclear bomb. For example, *The Naked and the Dead* (1948) by Norman Mailer (b. 1923) is still considered one of the greatest novels to come out of the war; it provides a narrow and terrifying view of the war, focusing on the lives of a small group of men fighting in the South Pacific. The brutality they experience and they themselves inflict is dehumanizing and soul wrenching. Yet, as Mailer himself says in his introduction to the 50th-anniversary edition of the novel,

> compassion is of value and enriches our life only when compassion is severe, which is to say when we can perceive everything that is good and bad about a character but are still able to feel that the sum of us as human beings is probably a little more good than awful. In any case, good or bad, it reminds us that life is like a gladiators' arena for the soul and so we can feel strengthened by those who endure, and feel awe and pity for those who do not.

Human dignity, indeed, humanity itself, must forever struggle in a world as grim as any nineteenth-century naturalist could conceive. Yet meaning and dignity are possible, Mailer suggests, if diminished and out of sync with the American dream.

Less literary than Mailer's tome is James Jones's (1921–1977) *From Here to Eternity* (1951). This novel, also written in a naturalistic strain, details the lives of military men in Hawaii just before the Japanese bomb Pearl Harbor. The central character, Private Robert E. Lee Prewitt, is shown struggling against a fate he cannot avoid. At the same time Jones portrays the inexorable forces of destruction, he, like Mailer, holds out hope for human dignity.

The third great novel of World War II is Joseph Heller's (1923–1999) *Catch-22* (1961). Written about World War II but during the escalation of the war in Vietnam, Heller's black comedy was so influential that its title has become a part of common, everyday language. The novel focuses on a bomber pilot Yossarian and his attempts to get out of the war alive. He can be relieved of his duties if he is declared insane, but if he declares himself to be insane to save his life, he must be sane and therefore must keep flying. The novel satirizes the utter stupidity and the absolute power of the military bureaucracy—and by extension the absurdity of modern life in a world ruled by bureaucracy in which the individual is merely a cog—a desperate, cognizant cog, in the machine. Heller's great novel is still read and referred to because it is the ultimate portrait of the absurdity of war; it applies equally to World War II, Korea, Vietnam, and even, some would say, to the conflicts with Iraq. It certainly influenced Kurt Vonnegut's (b. 1922) darkly comic look at World War II, *Slaughterhouse-5* (1969), as well as the wise-cracking and sometimes bloody humor of *M*A*S*H,* the film and later television series set in a mobile hospital unit during the Korean Conflict.

A direct descendant of *Catch-22,* and a work that reflected what some saw as the ultimate absurdity of the war in Vietnam, is Tim O'Brien's (b. 1946) *The Things They Carried* (1990), which not only reflects absurdity in its content but also exemplifies the POSTMODERN tendency to embody absurdity in form, challenging the conventions of novels mixing fact and fiction, blurring the line between truth and reality. The narrator is Tim O'Brien who is both the author and a fictional character. The form of the novel is part memoir, part short story—and its plot alternates between realistic action and fantasy. As with *Catch-22,* at the heart of the novel is a profound contradiction, an insane truth. The narrator, about to be drafted, considers dodging the draft by crossing into Canada. But, the narrator says, he was in the end too much of a coward to follow his conscience: "My conscience told me to run, but some irrational and powerful force was resisting, like a weight pushing me toward the war. What it came down to, stupidly, was a sense of shame." The narrator cannot bear to disappoint his family or community and elects to go to war. The real Tim O'Brien, opposed to the war, indicts himself as too cowardly to go to Canada in keeping with what his conscience tells him to do. O'Brien suggests that both acts were cowardly and motivated by shame.

Conformity, Rebellion, and Diversity

The America of the 1950s was a nation of conformists. Suburban neighborhoods were erected in which the houses were little boxes "made out of ticky tacky . . . Little boxes all the same." Corporate America enforced conformity in workers—in their appearance and in their attitudes. And mass media, including television and film, led to the creation of what many perceived as an empty, homogenous culture in which creativity and diversity were not tolerated. Of course, America was as rebellious and diverse as ever, and it was not long before the outsiders and the rebels began to assert themselves. The first of these was Holden Caulfield, the protagonist of J.D. Salinger's (b. 1919) *Catcher in the Rye* (1951), who finds the affluent life of postwar America pointless and, in his words, "phony." Holden was followed by a number of disillusioned outsiders, who in various ways and in various voices criticized American mass culture. Holden and all his descendents are themselves descendents of Huckleberry Finn, who can finally no longer tolerate civilization and must figuratively or literally "light out for the territory." These include Sal Paradiso, hero of

Vietnam War Memorial

Designed by Maya Lin, the Vietnam War Memorial in Washington, D.C., serves to recognize and honor those who served in one of America's most divisive wars. It was erected in 1982 and has more than 58,000 names carved into its black cut stone masonry panels. It is dedicated to honoring those who died in the Vietnam War, and, as the creator herself has said, "this memorial is for those who have died, and for us to remember." Visitors come from all over the United States to see and touch the Wall, and some etch names onto pages as remembrances.

🐌 THE LITERATURE OF THE VIETNAM WAR 🐌

The Vietnam War drove a wedge between generations and within age groups during the 1960s and 1970s. Those who supported the war, especially those who had lived through World War II, found themselves at odds with their own children, many of who felt that this war, in particular, highlighted everything that was out of balance in American culture. Not only was the imperialist United States interfering in what was, essentially, a civil war, but how the draft was structured ensured that those who fought and died were the poor, the dispossessed, and the uneducated—because exemptions from the draft were granted to those who held jobs vital to the war and to those in college.

At the same time, an intergenerational conflict arose between young people who opposed the war and young people who believed it was their duty to fight for their country. Returning veterans, who felt they had been heroes, were greeted with jeers and hatred by their compatriots who opposed the war.

With such conflicts at the root of the war, the literature that emerged from it was itself conflicted.

Much of the best writing to come from the war was penned by journalists and soldiers who witnessed firsthand the mismanagement and waste inherent in the conflict. Michael Herr's Dispatches *(1977) is often cited as the first work to capture the true pathos and chaos of Vietnam; Herr was a reporter for Esquire. Philip Caputo's A Rumor of War, published in the same year, is a memoir that traces the disillusionment of a young marine who volunteered out of patriotic idealism. The same disillusionment is particularly poignant in Ron Kovic's memoir,* Born on the Fourth of July *(1976). Kovic, a marine who volunteered for two terms of duty in Vietnam and who was paralyzed from the chest down, returned home in despair. It became clear to him that war, which he had once thought glorious, was, indeed, hell. Tobias Wolff's* In Pharaoh's Army *(1994), more distant from the war, is a sometimes very funny portrait of Wolff's own ineptitude as a soldier. The absurdity many perceived in the war was reflected in Tim O'Brien's* The Things They Carried *and in his* Going After Cacciato *(1978), the story of a soldier who decides simply to walk away from the war, as well as in David Rabe's disturbing play,* Sticks and Bones *(1973), in which a blind veteran returns home to a family that has an uncanny resemblance to the characters in a 1950s sitcom, Ozzie and Harriet.*

On the Road (1957); Randle McMurphy, hero of Ken Kesey's *One Flew over the Cuckoo's Nest* (1962); and many others.

The Beats

A number of young writers in the 1950s and 1960s, collectively known as Beats and including poets Allen Ginsberg and Lawrence Ferlinghetti and novelists Jack Kerouac and Ken Kesey, set out to transform America and American literature by experimenting with both form and content. Beat poetry was deeply pained and deeply personal in content and it rejected many of the formal strictures of earlier poetry. Ginsberg's *Howl* (1956) dispenses with rhyme, rhyhm and poetic diction, and replaces those structures with violent emotion. In a sense, the highly personal poetry of the beats was influenced by and influenced the confessional poetry by such writers as Robert Lowell, whose *Life Studies* (1959) is a monument to the importance of introspection, and, later, Sylvia Plath. Kerouac's *On the Road* (1957) dispenses with plot, for which he substitutes a freewheeling odyssey that blurs the line betweeen fiction and autobiography.

The New Regionalists

Perhaps in reaction to the image of America portrayed in the media of the 1950s and early 1960s, a new regionalism emerged. Southern writers, in particular, seemed intent on showcasing how truly different from the rest of the nation the South still was. Eudora Welty, Flannery O'Connor, and Carson McCullers, among others, created quirky, even grotesque characters, who either rejected or were rejected by the larger society. The subtext of much of O'Connor's work, for example, is the rejection of middle-class culture, including its lukewarm Christianity, which O'Connor sees as unworthy of the name of religion. In one of her best short stories, "A Good Man Is Hard to Find," for example, a hardened criminal, known as the Misfit, confronts a lukewarm Christian, referred to in the story simply as "the grandmother," with his atheism. Of Jesus he says,

> If He did what He said, then it's nothing for you to do but throw away everything and follow Him, and if He didn't, then it's nothing for you to do but enjoy the few minutes you got left the best way you can—by killing somebody or burning down his house or doing some other meanness to him. No pleasure but meanness.

Implicit in his words is the indictment of the grandmother, who claims to be a Christian but who is petty, mean, and not above lying to get her way. As he puts a bullet in her head, the Misfit comments in

> ### ৯ৄ MEET THE BEATNIKS ৯ৄ
>
> *Beatnik is a term that was coined by Herb Caen, a writer for the San Francisco Chronicle. Like the* EPITHET *Puritan, beatnik was originally intended to be derogatory but was quickly adopted with pride by those it purported to describe. The term, suggested by the name of the Russian satellite Sputnik, implied that beatniks were antiestablishment or even Communist and, in their own terminology, "way out." Beatniks worshipped "Beat" writers, such as Allen Ginsberg, Lawrence Ferlinghetti, Jack Kerouac, and Neal Cassady, who advocated eastern mysticism, freedom, the cult of the authentic individual, and defiance of authority.*
>
> *The caricature of the typical beatnik was a man wearing black, sporting sunglasses, a goatee, and a beret, holding a book of poetry or a woman similarly wearing black, down to her leotards, and heavy eyeliner. Beatniks had their own language—cool, daddy-o, dullsville, bread (money), pad (home)—and set of values, which later transformed into the antiestablishment attitudes of 1960s hippies. The typical hangout of a beatnik was a smoke-filled coffeehouse where poetry was read to the rhythm of bongo drums. The smoke was as often from marijuana as from cigarettes.*
>
> *The first beatnik to be portrayed on television was Maynard G. Krebs, who was one of the stars of The Many Lives of Dobie Gillis (1959–1963), a sitcom starring Dwayne Hickman and Tuesday Weld. Krebs, played by Bob Denver (who later played Gilligan on Gilligan's Island), loved jazz and hated work, shuddering whenever the idea of any kind of labor was mentioned.*

----

trademark O'Connor dialect, "She would of been a good woman . . . if it had been somebody there to shoot her every minute of her life."

Writers who wrote of life in the West after the war included Larry McMurtry—who punctures the image of the romantic West and the heroic cowboy—and his teacher, Wallace Stegner, whose work suggests that the wilderness of the West is a landscape uniquely qualified to develop true character. He says, in his "Wilderness Letter" (1960):

> Something will have gone out of us as a people if we ever let the remaining wilderness be destroyed; if we permit the last virgin forests to be turned into comic books and plastic cigarette cases;

if we drive the few remaining members of the wild species into zoos or to extinction; if we pollute the last clean air and dirty the last clean streams and push our paved roads through the last of the silence, so that never again will Americans be free in their country from the noise, the exhausts, the stinks of human and automotive waste.

Another of Stegner's students (he founded the creative writing program at Stanford University), Edward Abbey argued in both fictional and nonfiction works the urgency of preserving the western landscape.

The Jewish novel came into its own after the war as well. Many Jewish writers, including Bernard Malamud, Saul Bellow, Isaac Bashevis Singer, and Philip Roth, reflect the landscape of the urban North and deal with issues of assimilation—the extent to which a unique Jewish culture is being absorbed into the melting pot that is American and, hence, lost—and alienation—the sense of being different, of being an outsider. Roth's *Portnoy's Complaint* (1969), a brilliant comic novel that some considered pornographic in its depiction of the main character's repressed—and irrepressible—sexuality, was often criticized for its depiction of Sophie, Portnoy's smothering Jewish mother.

Feminists

Betty Friedan's (b. 1921) *The Feminine Mystique* (1963) ushered in the era of feminism. Friedan's manifesto begins,

> The problem lay buried, unspoken, for many years in the minds of American women. It was a strange stirring, a sense of dissatisfaction, a yearning that women suffered in the middle of the twentieth century in the United States. Each suburban wife struggled with it alone. As she made the beds, shopped for groceries, matched slipcover material, ate peanut butter sandwiches with her children, chauffeured Cub Scouts and Brownies, lay beside her husband at night—she was afraid to ask even of herself the silent question—"Is this all?"

Friedan's theory, as propounded in this seminal work, is that women were dissatisfied because they were forced to conform to an idealized image of femininity that was as unreal as it was unfulfilling. During World War II, many women felt liberated by working in jobs that had, until then, been the purview of men; when the war ended, these women were forced out of the work world and into the particularly confining mold of the suburban 1950's housewife. Not only did Friedan's work lead to more women writers and works with overtly feminist agendas—from the polemics of Erica Jong, to the ecofeminist works of Barbara Kingsolver, to the sisterhood of Alice Walker—but literary critics of the 1970s and beyond also began to demand a new look at the CANON of American literature, those works that are considered important by academics, literary historians, and literary critics. Until that point, literature by women had been considered inferior and outside the mainstream of American literature. But as academics began to examine the canon with a different set of lenses, nineteenth-century women writers, such as Charlotte Perkins Gilman and Kate Chopin, and twentieth-century writers, such as Zora Neale Hurston, were admitted to the canon—that is, they were included in anthologies, read in high school and college classrooms, and discussed by literary historians and critics.

As the canon accepted women writers, past and present, it also accepted multicultural writing. From the 1970s on, anthologies of American literature began to include Native American myth and poetry, the writings of early Spanish settlers, and the Chinese who labored on the railroads. The more such work was accepted into the canon, the more publishers were willing to risk publishing the work of Latino and Asian American writers who provide unique perspectives on the idea of the American dream. The story of how Latina writer Sandra Cisneros came to write *The House on Mango Street* (1984) is a fitting metaphor for the outsider/insider perspective that multicultural literature brings to American literature. As part of the creative writing program at the University of Iowa, students, Cisneros included, were asked to discuss the metaphorical implications of the idea of "home." In a flash, Cisneros says, she realized how utterly different her experiences of home and many other aspects of life in America were from those of her classmates. For Cisneros, "home" was a series of rented apartments in tough neighborhoods and eventually a ramshackle house, the first the family had owned. From these recollections was born *House on Mango Street*. Other notable Latino/Latina writers include Julia Alvarez, Esmeralda Santiago, Luis Rodriguez, and Gary Soto, who have brought not only new themes but also in many cases a new language into American literature. Similarly, Asian American and Indian American writers from Amy Tan to Maxine Hong Kingston to Anita Desai to Jhumpa Lahiri have begun to tell the story of life in America from their unique perspectives, which often include rigid social and religious strictures of traditional societies that clash with the openness and relative freedom of modern American society.

African American Writers

World War II had a profound impact on how African Americans regarded their lives in America. Many were disenchanted by the discrimination they encountered in the armed services, especially since they believed they were fighting to preserve democracy and the American way of life. In addition some soldiers experienced a startling and new sense of freedom in France, where they were not subject to discrimination and were largely accepted as equals—or even regarded as glamorous and exotic—by the French. After the war, however, returning soldiers encountered the same lack of opportunity and discrimination they had endured before the war. The anger and despair of African Americans found expression in several novels of the 1950s and 1960s including most notably Ralph Ellison's *Invisible Man* (1952), a harrowing tale of disillusionment in which the main character eventually comes to understand the dynamics of racism in America. With the blossoming of the Civil Rights Movement, African American literature exploded on the American scene, and writers as varied as Alice Walker, Toni Morrison, James Baldwin, Malcolm X, Gwendolyn Brooks, Maya Angelou, Amiri Baraka (LeRoi Jones), and others have written autobiographies and fiction that attempt to highlight the contradictions and the tragedy inherent in the African American experience.

Technology, Alienation, and the Absurd

Advances in technology have also influenced American literature in a variety of ways. Writers as varied as Don DeLillo, Donald Bartheleme, Kurt Vonnegut, and Thomas Pynchon have attempted to understand the impact that computers, television, nuclear weaponry, and other aspects of modern technological culture have on humankind.

Contemporary fiction tends to see technology and the resulting mass culture as a threat to humanity and to liberal values. The result, many of these authors conclude, is a profound sense of alienation and purposelessness. This sense of alienation often seems to lead to the absurd, a literature that is darkly comic and that tests the limits of form. Many postmodern writers question the meaning of contemporary life by calling attention to the artificiality of literature. Such writers include John Barth, Vladimir Nabakov, Kurt Vonnegut, and Richard Brautigan. If nineteenth-century literature tries to make sense out of life by telling stories that seem to have clear beginnings and ends, postmodern fiction attempts to make art as chaotic as life, by—as in Richard Brautigan's *A Confederate General at Big Sur* (1964), which

❧ THE UNIVAC COMPUTER ❧

Today, it is hard to imagine a time when there were no computers—and the size of today's laptops make it almost impossible to believe that the first computer to be commercially available, the Univac (which stood for Universal Automatic Computer), was 25 feet high and 50 feet long. The Univac, built by J. Presper Eckert and John Mauchly, was sold to the U.S. Census Bureau in 1951. The cost of developing the computer was close to one million dollars. Eventually, 46 were sold to government agencies and businesses. Eckert and Mauchly's company was purchased by Sperry Rand (later Remington Rand).

Computers have already had and will continue to have an immense impact on literature not only as a theme (Will computers take over? How will mechanization transform humankind? Can artificial intelligence compete with human intelligence?) but also as a device for disseminating literature. Thousands on thousands of texts are now available on the Internet and texts can be searched electronically for words and phrases. Some authors, such as Stephen King, have experimented with books that are issued only digitally, not printed at all. Dave Eggers, in the introductory material to his novel/memoir A Heartbreaking Work of Staggering Genius *(2000), offers to send readers an interactive CD of his work so they can change elements of the text. "This can be about you! You and your pals!" Eggers gushes, tongue firmly in cheek. But the possibility exists and no one yet knows what impact computers will have on the nature of literature in the future.*

---

has multiple endings that come faster and faster until it has "186,000 endings per second"—conflating the reader's expectations about the conventions of literature. John Barth tells stories within stories, writing as much about storytelling as about life itself. Nabokov focuses on wordplay and the artificiality of language and writes works of labyrinthine complexity, such as *Pale Fire* (1962), in which several levels of narrative complexity leave the reader dizzy and bewildered. These writers question the stability of the text along with the stability of life. Modernists who wrote before World War II questioned the meaning of life but still seemed to believe in art, in the idea that art itself could give life some meaning, that art, at least, had form and meaning. The purposelessness of life was something to be mourned. Postmodern writers, however, seem to celebrate chaos and fragmentation. Life is play and they play with art.

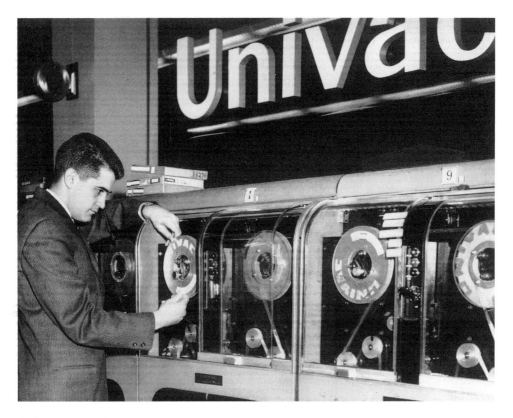

Univac computer
In 1946, the U.S. Census Bureau gave a deposit of $300,000 to J. Presper Eckert and John Mauchly to research and develop a new computer that was needed to handle the exploding U.S. population. After many delays and problems, the Univac (universal automatic computer) was finally delivered to the Census Bureau in 1951. As the better-known IBM had been a competitor of the Univac, the public was hesitant about Univac's capabilities. However, in 1952, in a publicity stunt, Univac correctly predicted the Eisenhower-Stevenson presidential race, quickly leading to its acceptance by the general public. The original Univac is now at the Smithsonian Institution.

2. THE FIFTIES

One way to think critically about the second half of the twentieth century is to begin with World War II and the effect its end had on American society. In 1945, American troops returned home from Europe and Asia to begin new lives and raise families. In response to this demand, William J. Levitt began building a series of neighborhoods in Levittown, Long Island, in which the inexpensive houses all looked, to some disturbingly, alike. Similar designs sprang up all across the country, and the modern suburb was born. In the beginning of the decade, many people felt as though America had left the chaos of the war behind and was returning to a sense of normality, which they largely welcomed.

It was with this post–World War II mentality in mind that J.D. Salinger (b. 1919) wrote one of the decade's most widely read rejections of these trends. *The Catcher in the Rye* (1951) tells the story of Holden Caulfield, a well-meaning adolescent who is unable to live up to the seeming promise of 1950's affluence and the conformity he feels it requires of him. In one telling episode, Holden discovers graffiti all over the walls of his sister Phoebe's school and realizes that no matter how hard he tries, he will never be able to recover his generation's lost innocence.

> I went down by a different staircase, and I saw another "Fuck you" on the wall. I tried to rub it off with my hand again, but this one was scratched on, with a knife or something. It wouldn't come off. It's hopeless, anyway. If you had a million years to do it in, you couldn't rub out even half the "Fuck you" signs in the world. It's impossible.

Unable to fulfill this or his larger dream of protecting children like Phoebe from entering into adulthood, Holden reveals his vision, which is based on a misinterpretation of the Robert Burns song "Coming through the Rye": "I keep picturing all these little kids playing some game in this big field of rye and all. . . . I'm standing on the edge of some crazy cliff. What I have to do, I have to catch everybody if they start to go over the cliff. . . . That's all I do all day." Holden's dream highlights the impossibility of his quest to preserve innocence in the modern world.

If Holden does everything he can to avoid the inevitable advancement of time, the America he describes does not. World War II produced many economic and cultural changes for the United States. After the war America occupied center stage as a world power. Almost overnight, the United States became a world leader in economics, politics, and popular culture, and American artists, musicians, and writers enjoyed a prominence they had never before known.

Having recently emigrated from Russia, Vladimir Nabokov (1899–1997) recognized the importance of documenting the developments in American culture from a foreigner's point of view. In *Lolita* (1955), his third novel in English, Nabokov tells the story of Humbert Humbert, a Russian professor who seduces a twelve-year-old American girl named Dolores (or Lolita) Haze. He takes the girl on a road trip across America and in the process discovers that, despite her childlike naiveté, she is actually quite experienced. At the same time Humbert's European brand of experience turns out to be a form of sheltered innocence that hides his own childlike neuroses. Nabokov's complex style suggests that there might not be such a thing as "reality." Instead, every individual uses such mediums as art, memory, imagination, and language to create his or her own version of events.

Although many aspects of the American experience seem odd to Humbert because he is experiencing them as a foreigner, the nation was undergoing such enormous changes in the late 1940s and early 1950s that most Americans could easily relate to his confusion. Many felt as though their own homes had become unfamiliar and foreign to them as well. Technologically, the wartime effort in the United States directly led to the invention of a number of useful products—such as Tupperware and Velcro—most of which we now cannot imagine living without. All of these technological developments—and many others—altered the average American's way of life and by extension the lives of nearly everyone else on the planet.

America Goes Global

A number of writers understood that the technological advancements of the 1940s and 1950s, which included, of course, the nuclear bomb, were not without their own set of dangers. In very different ways Norman Mailer's (b. 1923) brutal, haunting novel *The Naked and the Dead* (1948) and Kurt Vonnegut's dark comedy *Player Piano* (1952) each suggest that the common man is in danger of being destroyed by larger, often inhumane institutions. Although it takes place on the Japanese-occupied island of Anopopei, *The Naked and the*

Dead is less about the war itself than it is about Mailer's fear that the will of the individual might no longer be enough to defeat all of these new commercial, military, and political forces. As time went on, Mailer and later writers, such as Ken Kesey, Thomas Pynchon, and Don DeLillo, would come to believe that all of these different forces were all part of the same machinery—a vast, impenetrable, and unalterable MILITARY-INDUSTRIAL COMPLEX. No writer has been more consistently concerned with these themes than Kurt Vonnegut (b. 1922), whose novels and short stories pit ordinary characters against the absurdly bureaucratic or otherwise dysfunctional machinery of modern society.

More and more Americans began to travel abroad, and the government likewise began to focus more on the rest of the world than it had in the decades before the war. The biggest single threat to the United States in the aftermath of World War II was clearly the Soviet Union. In 1956, Soviet leader Nikita Khrushchev had declared, "History is on our side. We will bury you." Allies during the war, the United States and the Soviet Union found themselves competing for world supremacy as much of Europe lay in ruins. Shortly after peace was declared and while European national boundaries were being redrawn, the Soviets tried to cut off the German city of Berlin from the West at the same time as they exploded their first atomic bomb, thereby proving they had both the desire and the means to overthrow governments and control populations in the name of COMMUNISM.

President Harry S. Truman responded to these moves by outlining the Truman Doctrine. "I believe that it must be the policy of the United States to support free peoples who are resisting subjugation by armed minorities or by outside pressure." Later known as "containment," Truman's policy committed the United States to fight to stop the spread of communism anywhere in the world. Political theorists and government officials believed in the DOMINO EFFECT, the theory that the loss of even the smallest country to communism might cause nearby countries to also switch allegiances. It was this policy that directly led to the KOREAN CONFLICT in the 1950s and the VIETNAM WAR in the 1960s.

On December 8, 1953, President Dwight D. Eisenhower delivered his famous "Atoms for Peace" speech before the United Nations. Eisenhower proposed an international atomic energy agency and stressed the possibility for the peaceful development of nuclear energy. At the same time, the U.S. government was using nuclear technology to build more powerful hydrogen bombs. The atomic bomb

❧ NORMAN MAILER'S "THE WHITE NEGRO" (1957) ❧

One of the most important and defining works of cultural criticism in the 1950s was Norman Mailer's essay "The White Negro," in which Mailer suggests that the figure of the Negro provided an ideal model for the "white hipster." Mailer uses the terms square and hip to describe those individuals who easily succumb to the predominant culture's totalitarian teachings (squares) and those who (often criminally or "psychopathically") depart from them (hipsters).

Mailer argued that the treatment of the Negro in white society allowed him to experience American culture from outside. "Hated from outside and therefore hating himself," Mailer wrote, "the Negro was forced into the position of exploring all those moral wildernesses of civilized life which the Square automatically condemns as delinquent or evil or immature or morbid or self-destructive or corrupt."

Mailer suggests that the atrocities of war have instilled in his generation the very real fear of instantaneous death by atomic annihilation, or else a slower death-by-conformity resulting from larger governmental and societal forces. The solution for some, Mailer claims, is to embrace a form of mainstream cultural opposition by turning away from Square culture. By encouraging the "psychopath" in themselves, these hipsters turn out to share some commonalities with the Negro who has learned to cope under similar circumstances throughout the United States's history.

---

was seen as the biggest threat and the greatest deterrent to another world war. The ATOMIC AGE was born.

The United States and Soviet Union each moved quickly to establish geographical and political alliances with other nations. In response to these developments, Eisenhower, in his farewell address to the nation, warned Americans of the dangers of the growing military establishment and the arms industry. He said, "we must guard against the acquisition of unwarranted influence, whether sought or unsought, by the military industrial complex. The potential for the disastrous rise of misplaced power exists and will persist." He feared that the United States would increasingly come to be controlled by an alliance between the military and the businesses and industries that supplied it with its ships, planes, rockets, and arms.

Advertising America

Because the Cold War was largely a battle of ideologies, it became important for both democratic and Communist leaders to display the benefits of their way of life to the rest of the world. Both sides wanted to showcase the development of new technologies, particularly those that had military applications, which explains why the Soviet's launching of the *Sputnik* satellite in 1957 upset so many Americans and quickly led to the start of the space race between the two superpowers.

The "kitchen" debate between Vice President Richard Nixon and Soviet leader Nikita Khrushchev showed that even the relative standards of living between families in the two countries was a matter for intense debate. Televised before the world, the two men stood in a model kitchen featuring General Electric equipment in the U.S. Trade and Cultural Fair in Moscow. They debated such topics as women's roles and the relative advantages of modern American and Russian homes. Khrushchev was critical of American luxuries and asked Nixon, with a sneer, "Don't you have a machine that puts food in the mouth and pushes it down?"

With all the attention being paid to the status of the American family, individual families could not help but compare themselves to their neighbors. This phenomenon was known as "keeping up with the Joneses" after the title of a comic strip by Arthur ("Pop") Morand that ran in many U.S. newspapers from 1914 to 1958. The phrase was popularly used to describe the urge for suburban families to outdo their neighbors in CONSPICUOUS CONSUMPTION. This desire to have the best and newest products helps in part to explain the rapid rise of the television and automobile industries.

Mainstream popular culture was drastically altered in the American 1950s. The invention of the transistor helped make radio and television convenient and affordable to most American families and, as a result, television quickly became a household fixture. In 1945, there were only 14,000 television sets nationwide; by 1950, that number had risen to more than one million. Because advertisers quickly saw the potential that radio and television provided, it became common practice to monitor who was watching and listening. In 1950, Nielsen began to track television audiences; similarly, the "top 40" radio music format began in 1951. This of course meant that music and television shows now had to be popular to remain on the air. Being able to predict with some accuracy what was likely to be popular put pressure on writers and directors to provide only what the audience wanted,

🙠 Nixon and Khrushchev in the Kitchen 🙡

During part of their famous televised impromptu debate, Vice President Nixon and Soviet leader Khrushchev discussed the availability of modern technology to the average family in each country:

NIXON: This is the newest model. This is the kind which is built in thousands of units for direct installation in the houses. . . . Our steel workers, as you know, are on strike. But any steel worker could buy this house. They earn $3 an hour.

KHRUSHCHEV: The Americans have created their own image of the Soviet man and think he is as you want him to be. . . . All you have to do to get a house is to be born in the Soviet Union. . . . In America, if you don't have a dollar, you have the right to choose between sleeping in a house or on the pavement. Yet you say that we are slaves of Communism.

As Khrushchev is arguing, one difference between American democracy and the Soviet system is that under communism everyone is supposed to be guaranteed basic needs and equal distribution of resources in exchange for labor. The trade-off is that in a classless and stateless society one's labor is directly in service of the government. While Khrushchev boasted about the benefits of Soviet communism, the reality was that the standard of living in the Soviet Union was far more dismal than he let on.

---

sometimes leading writers to sacrifice their integrity and artistic vision to the demands of the marketplace.

In the novel *Wise Blood* (1952), Flannery O'Conner (1925–1964) perfectly captured the tension between authentic feeling and the pressures of marketing and advertising. *Wise Blood* tells the story of Hazel Motes, a would-be preacher recently returned from the Korean Conflict to discover that his heart is broken and empty of genuine belief in anything. Motes eventually discovers that no matter how hard he tries, he is unable to shake his most basic faith in humanity and as a result he ends up affirming nearly all of the beliefs he set out to reject. An excellent example of regional fiction and of the southern Gothic tradition, *Wise Blood* details the fracturing of the

American soul in the effort by some to modernize and mass market a religion whose core teachings resist such pressures.

American Responses to Un-American Activities

While the clash of ideologies between democracy and communism led to the Cold War (it is called this because no direct war between the two superpowers was ever fought), the fear that communism had already spread to America led to what is known as the RED SCARE.

In the beginning of the decade, two high-profile spy cases suggested that there actually were Americans willing to switch their allegiances and side with the Soviets. In 1950 a former State Department aide named Alger Hiss was tried for giving secrets to Communist spies. Two years later, Julius and Ethel Rosenberg became the first civilians to be sentenced to death for espionage, or spying. In response to these fears, Senator Joseph McCarthy held a series of pubic hearings between 1951 and 1954. Their goal was to discover those Americans who had connections to the Communist Party. Spurred on by McCarthy's investigations, the HOUSE UN-AMERICAN ACTIVITIES COMMITTEE (HUAC) also pursued those who were thought to have Communist ties. MCCARTHYISM involves accusing others of disloyalty or treason, while knowing that the accusations are false. Although many industries were investigated by HUAC, Hollywood became the best-known target.

Arthur Miller's (1915–2005) famous play *The Crucible* (1953) uses the Salem witch trials as a way to critique Senator McCarthy's own contemporary "witch hunt."

❧ THE KOREAN CONFLICT ❧

Unlike World War II and the Vietnam War, which continue to be analyzed for their impact on American life, the Korean Conflict is appropriately referred to as the Forgotten War. This may be partly because it was never actually recognized as a war by the U.S. government, even though roughly 54,000 Americans (nearly as many as in Vietnam and in a much shorter time period) were killed supporting democratic South Korea in its dispute with Communist North Korea. In reality, the United States and its allies were fighting a "proxy war" with the People's Republic of China and the Soviet Union. In the United States, the conflict was labeled a "police action" under the control of the United Nations rather than a war, which allowed officials to circumvent the otherwise necessary approval of Congress. Significantly, the Korean War was the first armed conflict of the Cold War and it set a precedent for many later conflicts. Most importantly, it established the concept of a "limited war," where the two superpowers could fight without involving nuclear weapons or directly attacking one another. It also expanded the Cold War's geopolitical range, which had previously been concerned mostly with Europe.

Joe McCarthy and McCarthyism

Joseph McCarthy (seated at desk, facing left) speaks to a group of reporters. In 1947, the House Un-American Activities Committee (HUAC) began investigating Hollywood's motion picture industry in a hunt for communists. By 1950, Senator McCarthy (from Wisconsin) claimed to have a list of 57 people in the State Department known to be members of the Communist Party. With the war in Korea and Communist advances in Eastern Europe, U.S. citizens were increasingly fearful of the potential of communism overtaking America. This anticommunist hysteria, and the accompanying modern version of a witch hunt, became known as McCarthyism.

Set in Salem, Massachusetts, in 1692, the play captures the terrifying consequences of accusation in an atmosphere of panic. In *The Crucible* Miller uses the fear of black magic to parallel fears about the power and influence of communism in the United States. In this way, the hysteria that leads to the execution of many prominent members of the Salem community is similar to the blacklisting that destroyed the careers and lives of many innocent people.

If Americans feared that communism might reach America, they were shocked to discover, on October 4, 1957, that it had reached outer space. Perhaps the single most significant development of the Cold War in the 1950s was the Soviet's launching of *Sputnik I,* the first man-made satellite. Although it was only one of the many developments in the decades-long competition between the United States and the Soviet Union, it alone had the impact of launching the SPACE AGE. The United States did eventually surpass the Soviet Union on July 20, 1969, becoming the only nation to land a man on the moon.

Witnessing the Invisible Man

Of course not everything happening in America in the 1950s was directly related to these international events. Probably the most important change occurring within the United States was the Civil Rights Movement, which began in earnest in 1954. In that year the Supreme Court said, in *Brown v. Board of Education of Topeka,* that the segregation of schools was unconstitutional. One year later Rosa Parks led African Americans to boycott segregated buses in Montgomery, Alabama. It was at this time that Martin Luther King, Jr., gained national recognition for his tactic of passive resistance, in which protesters engaged in nonviolent demonstrations to protest segregation and discrimination. By 1957, Congress passed the Civil Rights Act, which prohibited discrimination based on race, color, religion, or national origin. Simply changing the laws cannot put an end to discrimination, however, and soon after riots broke out in Little Rock, Arkansas, as nine African American students attempted to enter Central High School. Federal troops were then called in to escort the students to class.

African American writers such as Richard Wright (1908–1960), Ralph Ellison (1914–1994), and James Baldwin (1924–1987) had dealt with issues of racial inequality in their writing. Influenced by Fyodor Dostoevsky's *Notes from Underground* (1864), *Invisible Man* (1952) was Ellison's monumental tale of a nameless African American man's journey to discover and define himself against racist atti-

Death of a Salesman by Arthur Miller
This poster advertising Arthur Miller's Pulitzer Prize-winning play _Death of a Salesman_ was displayed at the Cape Theatre, in Cape May, New Jersey. Originally published in 1949, _Death of a Salesman_ portrays the tragic character of Willy Loman, a failed businessman who cannot revitalize his life. Also winner of a Drama Critics Circle Award, and a timeless story, the play is often restaged in theaters around the country.

tudes in both the rural South and urban North. *Invisible Man* was the first book by an African American author to win the prestigious National Book Award, and it launched Ellison into the national spotlight.

Invisible Man traces the unnoticed or "invisible" narrator through his childhood in the rural South, his days on scholarship at an African American college, and finally his involvement with the Brotherhood (modeled after Communist organizations) as an adult in Harlem, New York. In each of the novel's three sections, the narrator tries to come to terms with the strengths and limitations of being a black man in America.

Saul Bellow (1915–2005), a Jewish American writer and winner of the 1976 Nobel Prize for Literature, said of *Invisible Man:*

> I was keenly aware, as I read this book, of a very significant kind of independence in the writing. For there is a way for Negro novelists to go at their problems, just as there are Jewish or Italian ways. Mr. Ellison has not adopted a minority tone. If he had done so, he would have failed to establish a true middle-of-consciousness for everyone.

Bellow was one of a number of Jewish writers who took up the enormous task of writing about the European and American Jewish experience in the aftermath of the Holocaust. Like writers Phillip Roth (b. 1933) and Isaac Singer (1902–1991), Bellow explored themes of alienation and victimization in a world that found many Jews searching for answers and a new place to call home. In novels such as *The Adventures of Augie March* (1953), *Seize the Day* (1956), and *Henderson the Rain King* (1959), Bellow created characters obsessed with knowing themselves and discovering their intended place in the universe.

❧ THE KINSEY REPORTS ❧ AND PLAYBOY MAKE ISSUES OF SEX

Two main phenomena are considered largely responsible for the beginning of the American sexual revolution in the 1950s: the **Kinsey Reports** *and* **Playboy** *magazine. Together, these works caused enormous debate about the nature of sexuality and its place in the mass media. At that time, a man and woman could not appear in bed together on television. Instead, when a couple's bedroom was shown, it was common practice to feature separate twin beds, side-by-side. Additionally, there was absolutely no mention of nonheterosexual relationships anywhere on television.*

Alfred C. Kinsey's 1948 study **Sexual Behavior in the Human Male** *instantly became the biggest American bestseller since Margaret Mitchell's* **Gone with the Wind.** *More than 200,000 copies were sold in the first two months alone, thereby revealing that the American public was keenly interested in exploring the nature of sexuality. In 1953, Kinsey followed up the earlier reports with* **Sexual Behavior of the Human Female.**

❧ EXISTENTIALISM AND THE BEATS ❧

EXISTENTIALISM, a philosophical movement, became popular in France after World War II. The movement's most defining text is Jean-Paul Sartre's Existentialism Is a Humanism (1946), in which he famously argues that "existence precedes and rules essence." By this, Sartre means that the meaning of an individual's life (essence) is not determined by God or fate; rather, each individual defines him or herself through existence—the choices and actions that constitute a human life. By emphasizing individual choice and freedom, Sartre claims that, regardless of their situation or status, everyone experiences individual moments in which he or she is free to choose. With the gift, however, comes a tremendous responsibility to act not only in one's self-interest but also in the interest of all humankind.

Existentialism's emphasis on individual choice had an enormous influence on the American Beat generation writers. The term beat was coined by Jack Kerouac to describe the work of a generation of writers that included Allen Ginsberg, Neal Cassady, Gary Snyder, and William Burroughs. Kerouac intended the term to suggest a state of "exalted exhaustion" but which was also linked to the Catholic notion of a "beatific vision," one that was understood to be sacred and holy. Kerouac's own style was to tape together twelve-foot-long sheets of tracing paper so that he could type frantically without interruption. This form of "spontaneous writing," Kerouac believed, would allow him to overcome many of the socially imposed restraints that might otherwise limit his creative output.

New Mobility at the End of the 1950s

Alongside the Civil Rights Movement in the 1950s, a number of other major social changes were affecting Americans' attitudes about one another. Just as U.S. culture was exported to other parts of the world, so too did a variety of foreign products and ideas help to influence American society. Many minority soldiers returned from fighting in Europe with changed attitudes about their treatment in the United States. Particularly in France, African American soldiers were surprised to discover that they were treated with greater equality and respect than they had ever known in the United States. Partly for this reason, French philosophy and fiction enjoyed more exposure and influence among progressive U.S. thinkers after the war. In particular, the Existentialist work of Jean-Paul Sartre (1905–1980) and Albert Camus (1913–1960) influenced an entire generation of writers around the world and changed the way that many Americans thought about themselves, their choices, and some of the larger movements of world history.

At the same time, the BEAT GENERATION began to think seriously about Eastern philosophy and to incorporate its themes into their writing. The Beats were a group of writers who arose in the 1950s and whose central ideas took hold with the subsequent generation in the sixties. The Beats tended to value natural pursuits over technological or commercial ones, emphasized the importance of consciousness in shaping experience, and were almost exclusively pacifist. William Burroughs's (1914–1997) novel *Naked Lunch* (1957) and Allen Ginsberg's (1926–1997) long poem *Howl* (1956) were enormously influential expressions of Beat philosophy. The most famous of the Beat novels was written by Jack Kerouac (1922–1969). *On the Road* (1957) describes the desire on the part of some eccentric, romantic characters (modeled after some of Kerouac's own friends including the poet Allen Ginsberg) to recapture the lost soul of America somewhere along its lost highways.

3. THE SIXTIES AND BEYOND

Beginning with John F. Kennedy's narrow defeat of Richard Nixon in the 1960 presidential election, many young Americans felt as though they had found in Kennedy a trusted leader who would usher in a new era of opportunity. The Kennedy family captured the public's imagination like no first family had done before, especially in the television era, and the press began to refer to the Kennedy White House as Camelot, suggesting that it was as magical as the legendary home of King Arthur. If President Kennedy's youth and charisma signaled a change in the national outlook, his assassination in November 1963 marked its abrupt end. The remainder of the 1960s did little to calm most Americans' anxieties. The assassinations of Malcolm X, Martin Luther King, Jr., and Robert Kennedy followed in rapid succession. At the same time, under the leadership of President Lyndon B. Johnson, American soldiers were being sent off to Vietnam, more than 50,000 of whom would not return. In response to these events, the youth of America rebelled against what they called "the establishment," the adult world of business, politics, and the military. Known as the COUNTERCULTURE MOVEMENT, this youth rebellion led to revolutionary changes in music, clothing, and hairstyles, as well as daily habits and routines.

Internationally, the 1960s saw a great many colonies and territories—many of them in Africa—gain independence from their former European rulers. Elsewhere, the United States and the Soviet Union exerted tremendous influence over important regions of the world. The Eastern, or Soviet, Bloc consisted of Bulgaria, Romania, Hungary, East Germany, Poland, Albania, and Czechoslovakia. Additionally, the Soviet Union exerted influence over North Korea, Cuba, Vietnam, and the People's Republic of China. At the other end of the political spectrum, Western Europe, Japan, and South Korea were often said to be under the "sphere of influence" of the United States.

In conjunction with the success and failure of various claims to independence, both national and individual, many American writers struggled to define their own growing sense of freedom. The BLACK ARTS MOVEMENT drew from the example of African nations that had recently attained their independence to open up new artistic ground in the United States. The work of artists associated with this movement tended to be both political and artistic. Elsewhere, writers such as Adrienne Rich (b. 1929) and Philip Roth (b. 1933) were examining new topics in sexuality.

❧ THE FALLOUT SHELTER ❧

Popular phrases such as "Better dead than Red" suggested the awful possibility that the United States and the U.S.S.R. might actually go to war. One of the social phenomena that resulted from this fear was the fallout shelter, a self-contained unit that, in the event of a nuclear attack, was supposed to provide a family with food, water, and other supplies.

Tim O'Brien's novel The Nuclear Age (1979) *recalls the American preoccupation with the idea of nuclear war. The novel chronicles William Cowling's effort to dig a fallout shelter in his backyard. As the tale progresses, the reader discovers that Cowling is really seeking shelter from family obligations and the very real threat of nuclear war. At one point, Cowling recalls his childhood in the 1950s, when he made a fallout shelter using his Ping-Pong table.*

"The year was 1958 and I was scared. Who knows how it started? Maybe it was all the CONELRAD *[Control of Electromagnetic Radiation] stuff on the radio, tests of the Emergency Broadcast System, pictures of H-Bombs in* Life *magazine, strontium 90 in the milk, the times in school when we'd crawl under our desks and cover our heads and practice for the real thing. Or maybe it was rooted deep inside me. In my own inherited fears, in the genes, in a coded conviction that the world wasn't safe for human life."*

New Journalists Document the Revolution

Television news "came of age" with its reporting of President Kennedy's assassination in 1963. Subsequently, nearly nightly footage showed American soldiers wounded, dead, or dying in Vietnam. Beginning with the Nixon-Kennedy debate in 1960, policy makers and politicians came to understand television's enormous potential to change the public's mind.

LITERARY JOURNALISM also sought to capture the era in new and innovative ways. In response to escalating violence abroad and the remarkable number of social changes taking place at home, journalists looked for new ways to express themselves and the harsh realities they experienced. Journalists such as Truman Capote, Tom Wolfe, Norman Mailer, and Joan Didion increasingly began to use fictional techniques to supplement and craft the information they gathered.

❧ CHAIRMAN MAO, THE CULTURAL REVOLUTION, ❧
AND ANDY WARHOL

The United States was not the only country to undergo a significant cultural revolution in the 1960s. At the same time that the "flower children" of San Francisco were ushering in a new era of free love and experimentation, Chinese leader Mao Tse-Tung (or Zedong) was leading a very different sort of revolution in the People's Republic of China.

On August 1, 1966, the Chinese government passed "Decisions on the Great Proletarian Cultural Revolution," a bill that declared the government's support of a plan to rid China of intellectuals and imperialists. Most of these "purging" acts were committed by Mao's Red Guard. Most members of the Red Guard were children in their midteens who supported Mao's plan for a "classless society," in which every citizen works to achieve the common good. For Mao and his millions of Red Guard supporters, this meant brutally torturing and killing known members of the "bourgeoisie," or middle class, and anyone else considered a "counterrevolutionary," including teachers and politicians. By 1969, Mao dismantled the Red Guard, fearing that they would cause additional chaos and harm the Chinese Communist Party.

In the 1960s, American artist Andy Warhol made his reputation by painting famous American products, such as Campbell's soup cans and Coca-Cola. He then switched to silkscreen prints because he wanted not only to make art of mass-produced items but also to mass produce the art itself. Warhol's giant silkprint Mao (1972) seems to suggest that the artist himself might come to fashion a legacy as enduring as political icons like the Chinese leader. If one look closely, one can see Warhol's added brush strokes spanning the entire canvas, thus making Warhol as much the subject of the painting as Mao.

These writers believed that there could be no such thing as objective reality—simply choosing which facts to report, they claimed, was a subjective decision. Truman Capote (1924–1984) called works such as *In Cold Blood* (1966), his imaginative recreation of the true-life brutal murder of a Kansas family, "non-fiction novels," in that they blended factual information with common fictional approaches.

New journalism (as Tom Wolfe referred to the practice) was not invented in the 1960s, but the decade did see a tremendous development and increased application of the form, which was prompted by a broad range of political and social changes. Norman Mailer (b. 1923) has been one of the most consistently challenging and influential journalists and novelists to come out of the 1960s. In works such as *Why Are We in Vietnam?* (1967), *Armies of the Night* (1968), and *Miami and the Siege of Chicago* (1968), Mailer perfectly exemplifies the new journalist.

In *Armies of the Night,* Mailer focuses his attention on an actual march on the Pentagon, which represented an attempt by antiwar protesters to change government policy. Subtitled "Novel as History, History as Novel," Mailer includes himself as both a character in the work and as its SELF-CONSCIOUS NARRATOR. In this way, Mailer is able to capture perfectly the conflict between a massive large-scale movement of protesters and the mentality of a single individual who is both part of and separate from it.

All the Presidents' Crises

In the 1960s, three presidents oversaw one of the most tumultuous decades in American history. One of the best ways to understand the decade and much of the literature that has emerged from it is to profile these three presidents and the various conflicts that came to define their administrations. The decisions made by individual presidents, in turn, provide a useful way to understand the complex interrelationship of domestic and international crises and blurred lines between private and public identity.

John F. Kennedy (1917–1963)

The 1960s saw the escalation of the Cold War. A number of smaller conflicts developed in different parts of the world, suggesting that the Cold War might soon escalate into an actual war between the United States and the Soviet Union. In May 1960, the Soviets shot down an American spy plane over Russia. The United States' refusal to apologize for spying only intensified the already-strained relationship between the two superpowers.

Located just 90 miles off the coast of the Florida, Cuba became centrally important to the Cold War in the early 1960s. Since Fidel Castro's revolutionary rise to power in 1959, Cuba was considered to be a threat by the United States and an opportunity to nurture a Communist nation in America's backyard by the Soviet Union. President Kennedy responded to this danger by secretly ordering a Cuban uprising, the "Bay of Pigs Invasion." The result was a disaster; Kennedy backed out at the last minute leaving the revolutionaries, who were led by a group of 1,200 anti-Castro expatriates, to be tortured and killed. Then in August of that year, the Soviets attempted to establish missile bases in Cuba. Kennedy ordered a blockade, in which the U.S. Navy patrolled the Caribbean waters in order to prevent Soviet ships from delivering their weapons to Cuba. "The CUBAN MISSILE CRISIS" was a thirteen-day standoff between the United States and the Soviet Union that many people believed would soon escalate into a full-scale war. At the end of the standoff, the Soviets turned their ships back and the Western Hemisphere remained free of direct Soviet presence.

President Kennedy was assassinated by Lee Harvey Oswald on November 22, 1963. Because many Americans questioned Oswald's motives for the assassination and feared he may have been acting on behalf of someone else, President Johnson authorized the Warren Commission to investigate the murder. The Warren Report concluded that Oswald had acted alone. Nevertheless, the fear that the U.S. government had played some conspiratorial role in Kennedy's death, its coverup, or both, only served to further alienate many Americans from the establishment.

Lyndon Johnson (1908–1973)

On the same day Kennedy died, Lyndon Baines Johnson was sworn in as president. Johnson had hoped to put his energy toward the creation of a "Great Society," and, indeed, during his administration, Congress passed 90 of 115 of his proposals, including the creation of Medicare. But the Cold War intervened, leading Johnson to focus more and more on efforts to prevent South Vietnam from falling to the North Vietnamese Communist government. Johnson and his secretary of defense, Robert McNamara, oversaw the escalation of bombing campaigns in the region. The restoration of a draft meant that military service was not voluntary, and, in many families, sons, brothers, and fathers were sent to battle.

Not only did many people oppose the war in Vietnam but some Americans also questioned a system of exemptions to the draft that sent an unfair percentage of lower-class and minority men to their deaths. These oppositions left many soldiers feeling alienated from their own country. At the same time many protesters believed that they needed to highlight the inequalities in order to end them. Controversially, Muhammad Ali was imprisoned for refusing to participate in the draft after his application for "CONSCIENTIOUS OBJECTOR status" was denied by the Selective Service. Ali also opposed the war on racial grounds: "I am not going 10,000 miles to help murder, kill, and burn other people to simply help continue the domination of white slave-master over dark people the world over."

𝄞 Bob Dylan's "A Hard Rain's A-Gonna Fall" 𝄞

Singer/poet Bob Dylan (b. 1941) is known for such popular antiwar songs as "The Times They Are a Changin'," "Blowin' in the Wind," and "Masters of War," among many others, but Dylan also penned a brilliant lyrical reaction to the moment when the Cold War came closest to becoming a nuclear catastrophe. In the liner notes to 1963's Freewheelin' Bob Dylan, *writer Nat Hentoff quotes Dylan as saying that "'Hard Rain' is a desperate kind of song," then adds,*

"It was written during the Cuban Missile Crisis of October 1962 when those who allowed themselves to think of the impossible results of the Kennedy-Khrushchev confrontation were chilled by the imminence of oblivion. 'Every line in it,' says Dylan, 'is actually the start of a whole song. But when I wrote it, I thought I wouldn't have enough time alive to write all those songs so I put all I could into this one.'"

The song was not simply about nuclear war, however. Dylan also wanted to criticize the way that public fears are created and manipulated by the media. Dylan explains,

"The "hard rain" of the song is not, however, nuclear fallout. It's not "atomic rain." The hard rain that's gonna fall is the last verse, where I say "the pellets of poison are flooding us all"—I mean all the lies that are told on the radio and in the newspapers, trying to take people's brains away, all the lies I consider poison."

––––––––––

There were numerous literary responses to the Vietnam War and to war in general, ranging from the new journalism of Norman Mailer, to the black comedy of Joseph Heller's *Catch-22* (1961), to the loosely autobiographical science fiction of Kurt Vonnegut's *Slaughterhouse-Five* (1969). Even though Heller and Vonnegut's novels deal with World War II, the absurdity they depict was clearly influenced by Vietnam.

Richard Nixon (1913–1994)

While appealing to the SILENT MAJORITY, Richard Nixon defeated Democratic challenger Hubert Humphrey to become the 37th president of the United States. Before resigning during his second term, he created the Environmental Protection Agency, putting an end to

❧ THE MANCHURIAN CANDIDATE AND DR. STRANGELOVE ❧

In the aftermath of the Kennedy assassination, two American films caused many government officials to rethink the power of film to affect the popular imagination.

The first of these was John Frankenheimer's The Manchurian Candidate *(1962), starring Frank Sinatra. The thriller depicts a plot by U.S. Communist sympathizers to take control of the White House by brainwashing a Korean War veteran into assassinating the opposing presidential candidate. Though the plot was initially viewed as far-fetched, the film was subsequently suppressed following Lee Harvey Oswald's assassination of Kennedy because many people believed that Oswald had been brainwashed by Soviet communists.*

Dr. Strangelove *(1964) is Stanley Kubrick's bitterly satirical look at how nuclear technology overtook humanity's rational power to control it. The film depicts an insane Air Force colonel who dispatches bombers carrying nuclear weapons to destroy the Soviet Union. The film's release was delayed because of Kennedy's assassination. When the film was released, moreover, Columbia Pictures included a disclaimer:*

> *It is the stated position of the United States Air Force that their safeguards would prevent the occurrence of such events as are depicted in this film.*

Given the intensification of the Cold War following the failed Bay of Pigs invasion, the Cuban Missile Crisis, and the assassination of the president, the studio felt that the public would find Dr. Strangelove's *scenario to be all too plausible.*

———————

the war in Vietnam, and became the first modern president to visit China, thereby reestablishing a relationship with the most populous nation in the world. However, Nixon will likely be remembered most for the WATERGATE scandal, which led the House of Representatives to begin impeachment proceedings against him and caused him to resign from the presidency in 1974. Two *Washington Post* reporters named Bob Woodward and Carl Bernstein wrote a series of articles that documented President Nixon's authorization and coverup of the burglary of the Democratic Party offices at the Watergate office complex in Washington, D.C. As told in *All the President's Men* (1976), their story eventually led to Nixon's resignation and shook many Americans' confidence in the presidency as a whole. The scandal also demonstrated the power of the media to effect meaningful change and suggested that conscientious writers could use information gathered through investigative reporting in new and powerful ways. In 2005, the informant, famously dubbed "Deep Throat," who helped Woodward and Bernstein gather evidence for the story, was revealed to be Mark Felt, second in command at the Federal Bureau of Investigation (FBI).

Civil Rights, Black Power

Although the Civil Rights Movement began in the 1950s with the *Brown v. Board of Education* decision and Rosa Parks's arrest for refusing to sit at the back of the bus as required by law at the time, the movement intensified to include all-out civil unrest in the 1960s. African Americans led a fight for basic equality, using a number of different protest strategies. Martin Luther King, Jr., preferred a policy of peaceful resistance modeled after Indian social reformer, Mahatma Gandhi. Malcolm X, however, advocated rapid social change "by any means necessary." By the same token, not all civil rights activists had the same goals. Some sought the passage of an amendment guaranteeing equal status before the law and full assimilation into civil culture, whereas others wanted to topple the existing white power structure.

In 1963, King gave his famous "I Have a Dream" speech in front of more than 200,000 people during the March on Washington, D.C. That same year a black church was bombed in Birmingham, leaving four African American girls dead. In July of 1964, President Johnson signed the Civil Rights Act into law. This landmark law prohibited racial discrimination in public facilities, government, and employment.

❧ CAT'S CRADLE ❧

Cat's Cradle (1963) is Kurt Vonnegut's exploration of the madness of the 1960s culture-counterculture. If Eisenhower warned of the "military-industrial complex," Vonnegut similarly warns of a "scientific-religious complex," arguing that institutions are necessarily as weak as the individuals in charge of them.

The narrator of Cat's Cradle, a man calling himself Jonah, sets out to write a book about the day America dropped the atomic bomb on Hiroshima called The Day the World Ended. He discovers that Felix Hoenikker, one of the premier atomic bomb researchers, also discovered and gave to each of his three children a chemical called ice-nine that had the power to freeze water molecules; if used, ice-nine would start a chain reaction that would destroy all water on Earth. Jonah travels to the island of San Lorenzo, where he eventually discovers that, by pretending to be enemies, the island's dictator and its religious leader, Bokonon, are in cahoots with one another. Such delicate balances of power are shown to be as unstable as they are deceptive, as the initial desire to harness the power in nature, and to manipulate human nature for the good of mankind, each fall prey to the inevitable absurdities of postmodern life.

Gloria Steinem

Gloria Steinem, co-founder of *Ms*. magazine in 1972, is one of America's most influential, eloquent, and revered feminists. Her 1992 book, *Revolution from Within: A Book of Self-Esteem,* was a bestseller and has been translated into eleven languages. Her lifelong career as a journalist and writer reflect her active participation in political and social causes in the counterculture. Steinem has inspired girls and women to assert their rights, to fight for what they deserved, to take risks, and to defend the rights of others.

In 1965, Malcolm X was shot to death at a rally in Harlem, New York. Full-scale rioting began in Watts, a mostly African American area in southeast Los Angeles, on July 1, 1965. By the end of the decade, many of the civil rights activists' goals had been met (at least on paper), although many of these victories had come at a high cost of human life.

During this time, such works as *And Then We Heard the Thunder* (1963) by John Oliver Killens, *The Man Who Cried I Am* (1967) by John A. Williams, and *Dem* (1969) by William Melvin Kelley explored literature's overtly political potential. Ideologically related to the Black Power Movement, the Black Arts Movement became the most organized and politically influential response to the politics of race relations in America. The goal of these artists was to achieve a separation from the domination of American racism and to reinforce pride in the beauty and strength of blackness. The movement also inspired multiculturalism by suggesting that minority groups did not necessarily need to assimilate.

The Black Arts Movement began in 1965 when LeRoi Jones (b. 1958; changed his name to Amiri Baraka in 1967) moved to Harlem, New York, and founded the Black Arts Repertory Theatre/School (BARTS). Other cultural centers followed in the San Francisco Bay Area, Los Angeles, and Chicago. Jones, a highly successful playwright, publisher, and poet, announced in his poem "Black Arts": "we want poems that kill." By this, he meant that politically motivated art could do more than create beautiful or thoughtful images—it could also be used to interrogate unjust institutions.

The movement created the possibility for future African American writers to gain national attention and a larger readership. Alice Walker (b. 1944) and Toni Morrison (b. 1931), for example, began to look to the past as a way to provide context for more contemporary events. In novels such as *Meridian* (1976), Walker explores the relationship between whites and blacks in ways that deflect stereotyping and instead promote an ethic based on individual encounters rather than a set of preconceived notions about human beings and their behaviors. Her most famous novel, the Pulitzer Prize-winning *The Color Purple* (1983), uses a series of letters to suggest that the African American woman is treated as the lowest of the low in society because she faces both racial and gender discrimination.

Toni Morrison is perhaps the most successful writer to emerge from this era in which African American writers explored new means of expressing both their engagement with contemporary political issues and their interest in rediscovering their ethnic and cultural roots. In works such as *The Bluest Eye* (1970), *Beloved* (1987), and *Paradise* (1998) Morrison explores the connection between language, identity, and memory. Language for her includes not only everyday speech but also cultural symbols, lost names, slave spirituals, and African myths. The discovery of these hidden narratives often brings with it a sense of empowerment and obligation.

Morrison's *Song of Solomon* (1976) is one of the best novels to capture the conflicts between the Civil Rights Movement and the Black Arts Movement. The novel examines Milkman Dead's search for gold and the related discovery of his family's lost African heritage. During his journey, Milkman's closest friend Guitar mistakenly concludes that Milkman has betrayed him and his cause, and the novel ends in their mutual bloodshed. Guitar belongs to a secret organization called the Seven Days, whose objective is to retaliate for the violence done to African Americans by committing identical acts of violence against unsuspecting whites. In opposition to Milkman and Guitar's feud, Milkman's sister Pilate forms a MATRILINEAL community of women who derive strength and support from one another.

The Counterculture Creates Escape

The Electric Kool-Aid Acid Test (1968) by Tom Wolfe (b. 1931) examines the 1960s drug culture from the perspective of Ken Kesey and his Merry Pranksters. Kesey (1935–2001), the highly successful author of *One Flew over the Cuckoo's Nest* (1962) and the more sprawling and ambitious *Sometimes a Great Notion* (1964), "dropped out" in order to experiment with psychedelic drugs on a trip across the country in a painted bus to visit Timothy Leary, one of the earliest promoters of the use of LSD. Wolfe's book captures a significant moment in the history of the counterculture when the Beat generation came in direct contact with the hippie movement, and Kesey was at the forefront.

Kesey's own *One Flew over the Cuckoo's Nest* depicts the modern world as an insane asylum in which natural impulses have been regulated and controlled to the degree that people can no longer function normally. Kesey's act of true genius is to tell the story from the sometimes-fogged mind of Chief Bromden, a voluntary patient in the asylum who believes that something called the "Combine" controls all aspects of human behavior. Incarcerated in a bleak, mechanistic institution run by Nurse Ratched, Chief believes the Combine to be responsible for turning men into lobotomized and neutered servants. Randal P. McMurphy arrives and helps Chief to regain his Native American manhood and tell "the truth even if it didn't happen."

Like Chief's final rejection of the Combine, many Americans sought a similar form of escape through all forms of antiestablishment protest, including drugs, music, sex, and free speech. College campuses formed the epicenters of the countercultural movement. In Berkeley, California, Mario Savio launched the Free Speech Movement in a series of rallies from September 1964 to January 1965. His efforts ensured that university students would have the right to express their opinions and to openly protest without censorship. Elsewhere, at Kent State University, Ohio, four students were killed and nine others were wounded by the National Guard during an antiwar protest on May 4, 1970.

Drugs and music played a large part in the youth counterculture. The Beatles' appearance on the *Ed Sullivan Show* in 1964 launched "Beatlemania" and an onslaught of rock groups from England dubbed the British Invasion. Their music had a profound effect on the 1960s and beyond. Albums such as *Sgt. Pepper's Lonely Hearts Club Band* (1967) altered the contours of popular music, expanding the sounds and the themes. American bands, such as the Grateful Dead, centered in the famous Haight-Ashbury district of San Francisco, used their music to advocate the use of marijuana and LSD.

Rethinking Mainstream Culture: Roth, Updike

One problem with the popular slogan "Make love not war" was that many people who embraced it ended up turning love itself into another arena for conflict. From the feminist writing of Adrienne Rich to the exploration of Jewish sexuality popularized by Philip Roth's *Portnoy's Complaint* (1969), a generation of writers turned their attention to the topic of relationships in the wake of the sexual revolution. Betty Friedan's *The Feminine Mystique* (1963) explored the idea that many women were dissatisfied with the limited choices afforded to them by contemporary society.

Philip Roth (b. 1933) explores many of the same themes in American Jewish culture. In his early works, such as *Letting Go* (1962) and *When She Was Good* (1967), Roth examined Midwest American life. However, beginning with *Portnoy's Complaint,* Roth turned his attention specifically to the repressed sexuality of the stereotypical Jewish male who is emasculated by a domineering mother. Roth has continued to examine Jewish life in his fictional and autobiographical work. In what is perhaps the strongest writing of the

Civil rights march, August 28, 1963

In 1963, President John F. Kennedy proposed a new civil rights bill to Congress, one that offered federal protection for African Americans who wanted to vote, shop, eat out, and be educated on equal terms with whites. In order to show their support for the bill and to pressure Congress to pass it, civil rights groups organized a march. On August 28, 1963, the day of the march, an estimated 200,000 to 500,000 supporters showed up, making it the largest political demonstration to that date. The march is remembered mostly for the famous "I Have a Dream" speech, delivered by the Reverend Martin Luther King, Jr.

last decade of the twentieth century, his American trilogy—consisting of *American Pastoral* (1997), *I Married a Communist* (1998), and *The Human Stain* (2000)—captures the last half-century by examining the radical 1960s, McCarthyism, and political correctness, respectively. Roth's most recent work, The *Plot Against America* (2004), again stretches the limits of his fiction by supposing that famed aviator Charles Lindbergh, a known Nazi sympathizer, had defeated Franklin Roosevelt to claim the 1940 presidency.

Although many writers of the 1960s sought to alter mainstream culture, others, such as John Updike (b. 1932), embraced it so as to more fully depict its problems and its buried promise. Beginning with *Rabbit, Run* (1960), and continuing with *Rabbit Redux* (1971), *Rabbit Is Rich* (1981), *Rabbit at Rest* (1990), and *Rabbit Remembered* (2002), Updike established an international reputation by chronicling the life of ex-basketball player Harry "Rabbit" Angstrom. Rabbit often finds himself overwhelmed by responsibility and guilt largely because of his seeming inability to make decisions. Elsewhere, Updike has consistently focused on domestic, white, middle-class lives of consumption and moral decay. He has always had a special fondness for detailing the effects these tensions have on marriage and other relationships. Despite his characters' frequent downfalls and ineptitudes, and amidst the turmoil and chaos of the worlds they frequently inhabit, Updike declares in *Problems and Other Stories* (1979), "America is a vast conspiracy to make you happy." Here, his is a subtle yet powerful reaffirmation of the enduring humanity of the American experiment as it enters the era of postmodernism.

4. CONTEMPORARY AMERICAN POETRY

Two poets whose work spans the entire middle of the twentieth century are Robert Frost (1874–1963) and Carl Sandburg (1878–1967). Frost was essentially a pastoral poet, one for whom the countryside and nature held many truths to be explored. Although he tended to use fairly conventional forms, he was quite modern in his use of rhythm and meter, as well as in his use of everyday speech. Sandburg, however, was, to some extent, a poet of the urban experience. Like Walt Whitman, his focus was on the nobility of the ordinary person. His use of FREE VERSE and everyday language, so familiar to modern readers, were departures from poetic tradition at the time. In a sense, then, these two poets are emblematic of the shift from a traditional poetic sensibility to the modern one.

Confessional Poetry: Robert Lowell, Anne Sexton, Sylvia Plath

Although Robert Lowell (1917–1977) is often regarded as the modern founder of "CONFESSIONAL" POETRY, the concept goes back at least as far as the lyrical intimacy of Sappho, a poet of Lesbos, writing in the sixth century B.C. Contemporary confessional poems are characterized by their intensely personal subject matter. Largely autobiographical in nature, these poems constitute a major shift in American poetic thinking. In reaction to the commonplace practice of dealing with public matters, often from the perspective of a single individual or unnamed narrator who was largely indifferent to the events being described, Allen Ginsberg, Robert Lowell, and a great many others in the 1950s, turn their poetic attention inward.

Before World War II, many poets tended to avoid confessional poetry. By the end of the 1940s, however, critical thought encouraged a poet to pay attention to the private experiences, processes, and procedures that helped bring his or her work into existence. The emphasis on the life of the poet made his or her politics a matter of public discussion. This debate, in turn, tended to suggest that politics itself could be better understood by examining the psychological drives and urges of the artist more generally.

One common feature of the confessional poets is that they move away from philosophical or scientific discourse as the basis for truth. Instead, they look for the answers to their questions in the fabric of

❧ ROBERT FROST GOES TEMPORARILY SNOW BLIND ❧

On January 20, 1961, John F. Kennedy was sworn in as the 35th president of the United States. Before television, radio, and live audiences, Kennedy famously announced:

> *And so, my fellow Americans: ask not what your country can do for you—ask what you can do for your country. My fellow citizens of the world: ask not what America will do for you, but what together we can do for the freedom of man.*

At the president's request, the much-beloved New England poet Robert Frost had written a new poem entitled "Dedication," which he planned to deliver at the ceremony. However, when the time came, Frost discovered that he had been temporarily blinded by the sun's glare on the snow. He was no longer able to read "Dedication," and so he recited "The Gift Outright" from memory instead. This was an appropriate poem, in that it seemed to echo Kennedy's message about the nature of patriotism: "Such as we were we gave ourselves outright / . . . To the land vaguely realizing westward."

Frost, like Kennedy, was a New Englander. His poems are some of the most read and anthologized of the twentieth century. In a time when many poets experimented with new and often trendy forms, Frost remained a rigid structuralist. He is often admired for his ability to combine metrical forms and spoken idiom, and his folksy, plain speech has great appeal. However, this is not to say that Frost's work is simple; his poems are often layered with irony many casual readers overlook.

---

their own lives. They also tend to investigate their families as the primary objects of an autobiographical study. In particular, early confessional poets, such as Robert Lowell, Theodore Roethke (1908–1963), and Sylvia Plath, all wrote poetry of their own life circumstances. The two most influential early examples of confessional poetry are Allen Ginsberg's *Howl* (1956) and Robert Lowell's *Life Studies* (1959). *Howl* is less brutally confessional than *Life Studies,* although it is more shocking because Ginsberg is so quick to blame abstract social forces for his individual condition ("I saw the best minds of my generation destroyed by madness. . . ."). *Life Studies* created less of a spectacle but resonated more deeply. It also launched a generation of poets who were intent on examining gender

Sylvia Plath

An acclaimed poet and novelist who published her first poem at age eight, Sylvia Plath may once have been considered the young woman who had everything—beauty and brains, a great and recognized talent, and a family. However, contrary to appearances, one of her most recognized works, *The Bell Jar* (1963), is a loosely autobiographical novel about the slow emotional collapse of a woman. Here, Sylvia Plath is in Paris with her husband, Ted Hughes, in 1956.

❧ THE BLACK MOUNTAIN POETS, 1950–1956 ❧

One of the most highly influential groups of AVANT-GARDE *poets took up residency at Black Mountain College in rural North Carolina. They tended to be postmodernists who championed something called an "open field" approach to their poetry. This approach encouraged poets to experiment with and improvise new styles in a manner similar to the avant-garde musicians and painters of the day. Heavily influenced by the bebop music of Charlie Parker and others, the group held the status of poetic technique to be of the utmost importance. The movement's most important piece of prose was Projective Verse, which Charles Olsen published in 1950. Olsen argued that each line of poetry should largely be determined by the qualities of the preceding line. Their form depended on the individual line, each of which was designed to be the length of a breath.*

The Black Mountain movement included the poets Charles Olson, Robert Duncan, Jonathan Williams, Denise Levertov, and Robert Creeley. Guest lecturers to the school included William Carlos Williams and Albert Einstein. Creeley, who left for San Francisco in 1957, helped create a link between his former group and the Beat poets he soon joined. The Black Mountain Review's last issue, in fact, featured work by Allen Ginsberg, Jack Kerouac, William Burroughs, and Gary Snyder. As with their strong connection to the Beat poets, the Black Mountain movement also influenced subsequent movements such as that of the L=A=N=G=U=A=G=E *poets. This latter group served as the poetic embodiment of* DECONSTRUCTIONIST *philosophy in that they paid particular attention to the ways that ideas are formulated by language to produce meanings.*

---

roles, particularly in the context of families. To eliminate any uncertainty about the collection's focus, *Life Studies* includes an autobiographical essay by Lowell.

The most consistent theme in all of Lowell's writing has been the intersection of public and private life. His two most influential collections are *Lord Weary's Castle* (1946) and *Life Studies*. The tone and style of the works are quite different. The first is rigidly metered, which some critics see as a desire following the war to reclaim a faith in structure. The latter volume, by contrast, is much freer in its form. It places a greater emphasis on common speech and deals with less classically dramatic content. This shift in form coincided with the

🙿 THEODORE ROETHKE (1908–1963) 🙿

Robert Lowell converted from Protestantism to Catholicism before he wrote Life Studies. *(One can only imagine the effect it had on his "confessional" poetry.) Another poet often identified with the same school of poets is Theodore Roethke. Unlike Lowell's Catholic approach, Roethke's poems often exhibit a faith in animism, or the belief that all living things have souls. The following example, taken from* North American Sequence, *has Roethke contemplating the poet's presence in an already spiritually infused wilderness:*

> *I would believe my pain: and the eye quiet on the*
> *growing rose;*
> *I would delight in my hands, the branch singing,*
> *altering the excessive bird.*

Here, Roethke uses a few brief sketches to examine broader social and familial issues, as well as to comment on American history and literary traditions.

Many of Roethke's early poems were inspired by the greenhouses his family oversaw in Michigan where he grew up. Roethke was a careful and thorough observer of these lush, seemingly self-contained worlds. These childhood experiences fostered in him an intense belief in animism. Roethke eventually used these smaller locales to examine larger and broader landscapes in his poems.

---

exploration of more intimate topics. As personal as some of these poems are, it would be incorrect to think that they do not also contain within them complex and important political commentary.

"To Speak of Woe That Is in Marriage," one of the poems in *Life Studies,* is told from the perspective of a wife whose husband is an unfaithful alcoholic. Rather than succumb to the degradation of her marriage, she turns his desperation toward her own gratification: "Each night now I tie / ten dollars and his car key to my thigh. . . ." As personal as this poem is, others are equally public and political. "Inauguration Day: January 1953," for instance, sees the culture as being completely misguided in its current choice of president. Following Dwight D. Eisenhower's victory, Lowell writes, "and the Republic summons Ike [Eisenhower], / the mausoleum in her heart," as if to suggest that the public's will is also a form of memorialized death.

Sylvia Plath (1932–1963) is another highly influential poet of the "confessional" school of poetry. She was also one of Robert Lowell's most famous students. Plath experienced a childhood filled with both promise and anguish. By the time she began college, she had already published a number of poems and journalistic pieces, and in 1963 Plath published an anonymous novel, *The Bell Jar,* in which she describes a nervous breakdown as well as the six months she spent in a mental institution following a suicide attempt.

In 1956, Plath married English poet Ted Hughes. The couple separated in 1962, and shortly afterward, Plath began to write with an amazing power and confidence. At the end of these several months of intense work, Plath returned to London with her two children and shortly thereafter committed suicide. Despite her youthful death, Plath's poetry should not be seen as an extended suicide note. Rather, her poems are read today for their depiction of a woman coming to terms with her position as a woman in the modern world. These poems were collected and published as *Ariel* (1965).

One of Plath's most famous poems, "Daddy," shapes her ambivalent feelings toward her father into art. Particularly admirable is the way in which she is able to convey her own sense of loss even as she demonizes her dead father: "Daddy, I have had to kill you. / You died before I had time—." Throughout the poem, Plath aligns her father with all sorts of oppressive institutions, ranging from his occupation as an instructor to the sustained depiction of him as a Nazi soldier. In this way, her need to kill him symbolically offers many creative opportunities.

Like Sylvia Plath, Anne Sexton (1928–1974) also studied under Robert Lowell. And, like Plath, she was plagued by personal problems—Sexton took her own life in 1974, almost a decade after Plath. Perhaps tellingly, Sexton began writing poetry after her doctor suggested she write as an outlet for feelings of alienation and depression. The majority of her poems include a critique of women's social roles as well as emotional responses to her own life. As a way to challenge the conventional limitations faced by women, Sexton often affords her female characters more central and important roles in traditional stories. As with the poem "Her Kind" Sexton is continuously suggesting that, "A woman like that is misunderstood. / I have been her kind."

Always fresh and wildly inventive, Sexton captures what it is like to make worlds out of ordinary objects. In "The Room of My Life" she demonstrates how the trinkets in her room creatively combine to form new ideas and novel poetic forms,

Robert Frost and Carl Sandburg

One of America's most beloved and leading poets in the twentieth century, Robert Frost was a four-time winner of the Pulitzer Prize, for his works *New Hampshire* (1923), *Collected Poems* (1930), *A Further Range* (1936), and *A Witness Tree* (1942). His poetry is perhaps best described in his own words, "Poetry should be common in experience but uncommon in books." Frost's poems were traditional in language and style. Here, Frost sits with fellow poet Carl Sandburg (on the left), whose poems are written in free verse, varying rhythm and meter, and using everyday vocabulary and inflection.

Compelled to, it seems, by all the words in my
   hands
and the sea that bangs in my throat.

Poetry and the Other Mediums: Frank O'Hara and John Ashbery

As Gertrude Stein and many of the other High Modernists had done some three decades previously, a number of American poets in the 1950s became immersed in the visual arts. The most prominent of these poets were Frank O'Hara and John Ashbery. Both men were associated with the 1950s New York painting scene and their work captures the emphasis many of these painters placed on the process of making art as opposed to the finished product.

"We are made perfect," the experimental composer and musician John Cage said in 1949, "by what happens to us rather than by what we do." Both O'Hara's and Ashbery's poems often read as though they are exercises in this life philosophy. As such, their goal is less to reflect images and more to accurately describe the way in which they ingest and process many stimuli at once.

Significantly, these poets do not often distinguish high from low art forms and are as likely to write about a newspaper headline or the lyrics and rhythms of a popular song as they are to discuss a classic work of art. Both demonstrate the ways that environment affects thought, and they seemingly come to view their own poetry as products of, as well as commentaries on, their society. In this way, their poems are sometimes *about* the composition of their poems.

Frank O'Hara (1926–1966) is commonly associated with the New York school of poets. As a curator at the Museum of Modern Art in New York City and a great admirer of painting, O'Hara tended to promote artists rather than criticize them in his work. In "Why I Am Not a Painter," O'Hara explicitly turns his attention to the relationship between poetry and the visual arts. He explains that in poetic form orange is not simply a color but rather an occasion to think of other things, like life. Elsewhere, O'Hara makes use not of the difference between poet and painter but of the relationship between two poets and their use of a similar figure of speech. In "A True Account of Talking to the Sun at Fire Island," for example, O'Hara imagines that he is only the second poet ever to be wakened by the sun (the other is the Russian poet Mayakofsky). The two poets, then, are imagined to be connected by their relationship with the sun, rather than by the deliberate evocation of the one by the other.

❧ JOHN CAGE (1912–1992): ❧
THE INTERDISCIPLINARY ARTIST

Perhaps no other postmodern artist has had as much influence on as many different art forms as John Cage. From music, to dance and choreography, to poetry and prose, Cage's work has produced significant innovations and extended the boundaries of nearly all modern media. Perhaps the most lasting contribution of all is the way in which Cage's work suggests that each of these fields has more in common than previously imagined.

One of Cage's compositional innovations was to organize musical structures based on the concept of time, an idea he derived from studying choreography and dance, particularly that of his lifelong collaborator, dancer, and choreographer Merce Cunningham. In another phase he attempted to translate the eight central emotions of Indian religion into music based largely on the notion of quiet. This burgeoning interest in the aesthetics of silence had a profound effect on Cage's later, more influential work. By experimenting with chance operations, Cage continued to develop his definition and use of silence in such works as Music of Changes *(1951) and* Imaginary Landscape No. 4 for 12 Radios *(1951).*

The publication of Cage's personal philosophy, Silence: Lectures and Writings *(1961), represented another shift in his career as his compositional interest in music began to wane. In addition to essays, his 1967 follow-up collection of writing,* A Year from Monday, *also contains poetry and social commentary.*

One of O'Hara's most celebrated poems, "The Day Lady Died" (1959), is occasioned by the death of Billie Holiday, a famous blues singer. The poem, unlike the traditional elegy, does not suggest that the world mourns Holiday's death. In fact, the world goes on just as usual: "I walk up the muggy street beginning to sun / and have a hamburger and a malted." But the memory of Holiday whispering a song "along the keyboard" makes the poet "stop breathing." Her art punctuates the moment and gives her life and the moment a special significance.

Like O'Hara, John Ashbery (b. 1927) is often associated with the abstract painting of the 1940s and 1950s. Yet his long poem *Self-Portrait in a Convex Mirror* (1975) has as its subject a Renaissance painting by Francesco Parmagianino and deals playfully with the old idea that the eyes are the mirror of the soul. Ashbery demurs, suggesting that Parmagianino's "eyes proclaim / That everything is surface. The surface is what's there." Even more so than O'Hara, Ashbery attempted to reproduce the rhythm and structure of thought in his work and in so doing influenced much of contemporary poetry. His first collection of poems was *Some Trees* (1956). In it, Ashbery appears to talk his way through the confusion of ordinary experience. Ashbery often jokes about the material he uses, as with "Instruction Manual," which is a catalog of clichés ordered to create effects. In a later poem, "Daffy Duck in Hollywood," he even ridicules his own previous work in *Self-Portrait in a Convex Mirror* by imagining it to be delivered by the cartoon character. Ashbery's goal, he claims, is to manipulate the language that most obviously captures our feelings, the language of everyday life.

By chronicling the impact that postwar capitalism and advertising culture has had on the poet's mind, Ashbery explores the relationship between the external world and our ability to internalize it. Ashbery concludes that American society leads individuals to feel alienated. Thus, there are few authentic narratives left to be told. Convention, for Ashbery, has become as commonplace as it is destructive.

Poem as Vision, Poet as Activist: Gwendolyn Brooks, Adrienne Rich, Rita Dove, Martin Espada

A number of postwar poets have created poetry that speaks to popular social and political movements. This does not necessarily mean that their poetry is consumed by these topics. Instead, part of their enormous impact has resulted from their refusal to limit the scope of their poems exclusively to these issues. In other words, they do not treat their politics in isolation; they instead understand their commitment to social and political change to be one part of a larger, organic way of interacting with the world. As we shall also see, sometimes not delivering on a reader's expectations can be the most political act of all.

Gwendolyn Brooks (1917–2000) grew up in Chicago, where she received training in both traditional and modern poetry. She also studied under Langston Hughes, one of the twentieth century's most influential African American poets. Because she possessed a wide range of skills, Brooks was able to write in a multiplicity of forms and traditions. She also became involved in the Black Arts Movement.

Brooks's poetry itself often considers international themes in local settings, most often those of the Chicago neighborhood of her upbringing. By blending features of modernist poetry with the language of everyday speech, Brooks is able to comment on the larger questions of race in America in a way that appeals to hard-line conservative poets as well as those with a more POPULIST outlook.

In "Of De Witt Williams on His Way to Lincoln Cemetery," for example, Brooks depicts the funeral procession of a "plain black boy" on his way to be buried in Lincoln Cemetery, a symbolic location because of its connection to the Great Emancipator. Brooks uses a regular rhyme scheme and also includes lyrics from a popular African American spiritual in order to invest the ordinary funeral of this ordinary boy with the solemn dignity and beauty often reserved for the great and famous. The poem seems to evoke Whitman's description of Lincoln's funeral procession in "When Lilacs Last in the Dooryard Bloomed,"

> Coffin that passes through lanes and streets,
> Through day and night, with the great cloud darkening the
>   land,
> With the pomp of the inloop'd flags, with the cities draped
>   in black,
> With the show of the States themselves, as of crape-veil'd
>   women, standing,

An ordinary boy, yes, but his death matters very much indeed.

Adrienne Rich (b. 1929) was born in Baltimore. Although she began as a formalist, Rich soon dispensed with traditional forms in favor of a more expressive and personalized delivery. Over the years, Rich has become an outspoken feminist and gender critic.

One of Rich's early poems provides a powerful illustration of these themes. The brief "Aunt Jennifer's Tigers" juxtaposes one woman's desire to be creative and free with the weight and burden of her expected gender roles, as when, "The massive weight of Uncle's wedding band / Sits heavily on Aunt Jennifer's hand." Here, we can see the symbolic burden that Aunt Jennifer's marriage places on her private and personal creativity. The ring is so "heavy," in fact, that she finds it difficult to sew.

Of all Rich's works, *The Will to Change* (1971) and *Diving into the Wreck* (1973) have had the greatest social impact. The former is arguably her most political, whereas the latter is the volume in which she first made explicit her feminist views. As in "Aunt Jennifer's Tigers," Rich is able to take a feminist theme and ally it to a related question about the role of the artist and the ability of the poet to make meaningful art that lasts.

In addition to writing poetry, Rich has also published a number of volumes of social criticism. In the wake of the very unpopular Vietnam War, the increased attention paid to poets such as Rich not only helped facilitate the success of *Of Woman Born* (1976), her first volume of prose, but also it more generally suggested that poetry might come to play an increased role in public debate.

The poetry of Rita Dove (b. 1952) is as much a celebration of African American rhythms and forms as it is an attempt on the part of the poet to distance herself from them. Dove's poetry is sometimes characterized by its intentional flatness, which is a refusal on her part to make the content of her poems lyrical. Instead, Dove prefers to craft an authority of her own, through her own structures and rhythms. As with the recollection of a mother's work as a seamstress to fund her education in business, "My Mother Enters the Work Force," Dove's own poetry is adept at, "traveling the lit path of the needle / through quicksand taffeta." In other words, she is able to thread her own way through the pitfalls of tradition.

Likewise, Dove's own poems do not easily fall into the bodily driven movements of the jazz- and spiritual-infused poetry of her predecessors. For this reason, Dove's poems might best be read in the context of the poet's own gender and race, though not necessarily as a product of them. Not only has her work been awarded the Pulitzer Prize (for 1986's *Thomas and Beulah*) but Dove also served as Poet Laureate of the United States from 1993 to 1995.

Of Puerto Rican descent, Martin Espada (b. 1957) was raised in Brooklyn, New York. After working in a number of different jobs including as a journalist in Nicaragua and as a tenant lawyer, Espada settled down to teach at the University of Massachusetts, where he has been involved in promoting and editing the work of young Latino poets. He is also the author of several volumes of poetry, most of which deal with political topics in a bold and funny style.

In "Bully," for example, Espada comments on America's conquest of Latin America through his description of a statue of Teddy Roosevelt, the former president who led a voluntary army during the Spanish American War. Humorously documenting the changing climate in which Roosevelt's past actions are now judged, Espada writes, "But now the Roosevelt School / is pronounced Hernandez." "Bully" appears in *Rebellion Is the Circle of a Lover's Hands* (1990), a volume that examines the relationship between the sort of action and activism he expressed in his own work as a tenant lawyer, and the interpersonal relationships that provide each of us with the comfort and support to continue.

❧ THE POET LAUREATE ❧

The Poet Laureate is an honorary position granted to one American poet by the Library of Congress. The position was officially established in 1986, replacing the position of Consultant in Poetry to the Library of Congress. During his or her term, the nominated poet "serves as the nation's official lightning rod for the poetic impulse of Americans. During his or her term, the Poet Laureate seeks to raise the national consciousness to a greater appreciation of the reading and writing of poetry." Because the Poet Laureate is an official government position, the poets chosen tend to be somewhat conservative in their approach to poetry.

Each poet brings a particular emphasis to the office. For example, Rita Dove brought together and supplied a public forum for poets of the African diaspora to discuss their work. Robert Pinsky, who served two terms (from 1997–2000), sought to make poetry an accessible and vibrant part of the digital age by encouraging the exchange and publication of poetry on the Internet.

Poet Laureates
(since the position was officially renamed as such in 1986)
Robert Penn Warren, 1986–1987
Richard Wilbur, 1987–1988
Howard Nemerov, 1988–1990
Mark Strand, 1990–1991
Joseph Brodsky, 1991–1992
Mona Van Duyn, 1992–1993
Rita Dove, 1993–1995
Robert Hass, 1995–1997
Robert Pinsky, 1997–2000
Special Bicentennial Consultants, 1999–2000:
Rita Dove, Louise Glück, and W. S. Merwin
Stanley Kunitz, 2000–2001
Billy Collins, 2001–2003
Louise Glück, 2003–2004
Ted Kooser, 2004–

Reading Espada's work, one is deeply moved by his concern for the power of language to wage a form of cultural war against the status quo and against a history of cruel injustice. In the recent collection, *Imagine the Angles of Bread* (1996), Espada continues to challenge many readers' assumptions about the nature of Hispanic culture and belief by evoking emotions as diverse as anger and humor as with the title piece's opening line, the first of many such imagined upheavals of the status quo: "This is the year that squatters evict landlords."

Poetry of Witness: Carolyn Forché

Carolyn Forché's (b. 1950) recent poetry anthology, *Against Forgetting: Twentieth-Century Poetry of Witness* (1993), is a perfect example of how bringing poems together can highlight common themes where we never thought to look for them before. In the case of *Against Forgetting,* Forché decided to bring together poems from around the world that examined the relationship between private and public, or poetic and political, spaces. "POETRY OF WITNESS" seeks to create a third space called the "social." It is meant to bring together public and private themes and to create a mode for them to interact creatively and beneficially. Forché's own *The Country Between Us* (1981) is a collection of poems that, in part, describe the violent and corrupt practices of the El Salvadorian military.

One effect of poetry of witness is that it is often highly subjective and deeply psychological in that these poets are very much concerned with the effects of having witnessed or experienced the atrocities they describe in their poems. Because narratives of war are so often told exclusively by the victors, it is important that such poems of witness be created to represent the opposing side. Forché's own "The Colonel" captures this need. Following her meeting with a Salvadorian military officer who emptied a bag full of severed human ears onto the ground, she writes, "Some of the ears on the floor caught th[e] scrape in his voice. Some of the ears on the floor were pressed to the ground." In this way, a single poem is sometimes all that stands between memory and oblivion.

5. NEW VOICES

In truth, there is really nothing "new" about ethnic literature such as *House of Dawn* by N. Scott Momaday or *The Joy Luck* Club by Amy Tan. What is new, however, is the attention now being paid to such works. Thus, one must ask, why has this literature only recently received the kind of broad readership traditionally enjoyed by European American and, to a lesser degree, African American writers?

The New Ethnicity

Beginning in the 1960s, thinkers such as Stuart Hall began to offer some alternatives to old-school ideas about ETHNICITY, ideas that were largely sociological and tended to describe individuals according to their race. In *Beyond Borders,* for example, Hall tried to rethink ethnicity along postmodern lines. Hall argued that globalization has in part allowed for new possibilities in our understanding of ethnicity. Rather than being something ahistorical and fixed, Hall argued that ethnicity should instead be seen as something temporal and changing. According to this concept, one's identity is a matter of choice—a diverse, political concept, rather than a fixed certitude imposed from the outside.

One important result of the new thinking about ethnicity has been the greater consideration paid to people of mixed race. These individuals are now less likely to be forced into one particular category, thereby officially denying one or more aspects of their backgrounds and self-identities. Once race and ethnicity are no longer believed to be determining factors in one's behavior, there is less incentive to label people.

Recently, theorists such as David Hollinger have suggested that those who are interested in supporting diversity need to move beyond multiculturalism toward something he calls the POSTETHNIC. He uses the term to describe a set of voluntary associations based on shared appreciation for a particular culture's practices and values, rather than strict ethnic membership in it. Rather than using the term *identity* to describe a person's orientation to the world, Hollinger prefers the term *affiliation*. Postethnic theorists believe that this difference is important because it suggests that individuals are not limited by any sort of ESSENTIALISM. In other words, they are free to choose which aspects of their backgrounds they would like to emphasize and further explore.

The Ethnic Canon

With the rise of "new ethnic" thinking in America, there also has been a greater emphasis placed on the work of different ethnic writers as well as a desire to see their contributions taught in American schools. Ethnic literature refers to works by minority writers, particularly those novels and short stories that deal specifically with the experience of being a minority in America. Critics who would like to see the canon represent more work by ethnic writers argue that too much attention has historically been paid to white male authors. They see these works as important, but they also argue that reading *only* these books does not allow one to experience the full range of American life. The American literary tradition is much more interesting, challenging, and diverse than the average high school or college curriculum might suggest.

In 1995, David Palumbo-Liu edited a volume of essays describing the institutionalization of minority literature. Called *The Ethnic Canon: Histories, Institutions, and Interventions,* the goal of the volume is to understand how and why certain works by minority writers achieve mainstream popularity, whereas others do not. The collected essays together argue that only the least challenging or controversial works become acceptable to teach, and that the extremely original and sometimes uncomfortable ideas tend to be overlooked or deemphasized. In other words, instructors are much more likely to teach a book that agrees with their own opinions than one that challenges them.

Ethnic Autobiography

One consistently popular form of ethnic writing is the "ethnic autobiography." Ethnic autobiographies often make use of oral traditions and popular cultural rituals in order to create a connection with the past. In this way, the individual can speak for a larger group at the same time that he or she can achieve membership in the group. This use of multiple voices is only one way that ethnic autobiographers universalize the particular and particularize the universal. Many ancestors can speak through one person at the same time, and it is often the incompatibility of their wishes that causes tension in the current moment. Additionally, however, this "collective sense of self" can be a source of tremendous strength.

There is a great range of possible approaches and uses for the autobiographical form. In *The Woman Warrior* (1976) and *The Fifth Book of Peace* (2003), for example, Maxine Hong Kingston analyzes her own childhood memories alongside broader Chinese traditions and myths not only in order to understand her identity as a Chinese American but also to bring the history of Chinese thought to bear on American culture. Although it is also autobiographical, the work of Gloria Anzaldua (1942–2004) is quite different in its methods and aims. Her goal is not to understand herself but to change the opinions of those around her. She accomplishes this through an unwavering belief that it is the culture and not the individual that must change. "I will have my voice," she says, "I will overcome the tradition of silence."

Finally, speaking from a Native American perspective, N. Scott Momaday (b. 1934) explains that his own voice is inevitably made from "the voices of my parents, of my grandmother, and others. Their voices, their words, English and Kiowa—and the silences that lie about them—are already the element of my mind's life." Assimilation is one of the more prevalent topics of interest in ethnic autobiography. On the one hand, many immigrants would like to blend in fully with their peers, even if it means the loss of their own culture. On the other hand, some people would prefer to maintain the cultural traditions of their native country, even if it requires isolation and alienation from mainstream American society.

Autobiographical elements also appear in nonfiction ethnic writing. Critics such as Patricia Williams have argued that one of the problems with mainstream culture is that it tends to silence the voices and ideas of minority writers. As a way to oppose this trend, Williams and others include themselves in their critical essays. This strategy is only one way to include ethnic writers and the topic of ethnicity in a broad range of scientific, philosophical, and literary debates.

The Native American Tradition: N. Scott Momaday, Leslie Marmon Silko

Even before a collection of the highly influential spiritual teachings of a Lakota healer, *Black Elk Speaks,* was first published in 1932 there had been significant interest both in translating oral traditions into written form and in translating existing Native American texts into English. Particularly since the 1960s, when Native American ways were explored as a viable alternative to mainstream American society, readers have become more open to works by Native Americans.

In 1969, N. Scott Momaday became the first Native American to win the Pulitzer Prize. *House Made of Dawn* (1968), his first novel, was an overwhelming critical and popular success. The novel ð **Vine Deloria (b. 1933) Declares, "God Is Red"** ð

Vine Deloria's important study of Christianity's influence on Native American culture, God Is Red, *offers a history of Native American activism against the U.S. government's racist policies. Deloria was a Native American author, critic, and political activist who influenced a great number of subsequent writers, including Leslie Marmon Silko.*

In God Is Red, *Deloria wonders how things might have gone differently if Martin Luther King, Jr., had been "red" instead of black. Would his equally legitimate claims to inequality have gone largely overlooked? Against these speculations, Deloria examines the actual relationship between the 1960s counterculture and the Native American struggle for equal treatment. He argues that the end of the Civil Rights Movement, the United States's involvement in Vietnam, and the increasing experimentation with drugs created a strong desire for "authenticity" that many whites believed the Native American culture could provide. Native Americans were optimistic that such interest in their beliefs and customs would translate into greater political recognition.*

The failure of this hope to manifest itself in legitimate social change led to the 1972 occupation of the Bureau of Indian Affairs offices in Washington, D.C., by a group of Native Americans who traveled across the country to protest the continued oppressive treatment of their people in the aftermath of the Civil Rights Movement, which they believed had overlooked them. The group, calling themselves the Trail of Broken Treaties Caravan, was unsuccessful in bringing about the changes for which they had hoped, Deloria concludes, largely because most Americans failed to comprehend their way of life or the particular history of their grievances.

---

describes a Native American named Abel who returns to his homeland after fighting a foreign campaign during World War II. Abel finds himself caught between the traditional life of his people and the postwar urban boom that represents both the possibility and the danger of leaving his people. This essential conflict—between a set of ideal values and the reality of living in a corrupt and alluring world—is one to which many Americans could easily relate. As Momaday himself explained, the people he met as a boy displayed "a certain beauty and strength that I find missing in the modern world at large."

Momaday's own life can be said to have contained some of the same contradictions Abel faces. When Momaday was growing up, both his parents worked as teachers on a nearby reservation. This gave him exposure not only to the Kiowa traditions of his father's family but also to many other Southwest Native American traditions. Momaday early developed an interest in literature, especially poetry. After publishing *House Made of Dawn,* Momaday moved to the University of California at Berkeley where he designed a graduate program in Indian Studies. His memoir, *The Names,* appeared in 1976. *In the Presence of the Sun* (1991) is a collection of stories and poems representing more than 30 years of Momaday's work and includes drawings and paintings by the artist.

Momaday's unprecedented success made possible the careers of other Native American writers, including Leslie Marmon Silko, James Welch, and Sherman Alexie. Of these three, the best known is Silko (b. 1948), author of several novels including *Ceremony* (1977), *Storyteller* (1981), *Almanac of the Dead* (1991), and her most recent *Gardens in the Dunes* (1999). In *Almanac of the Dead,* Silko attempts to provide an alternative moral history of the Americas. In it, she condemns whites for their treatment of the Native Americans and the land. According to Silko's retelling, the conquered peoples will soon have their revenge in the form of the second coming of the Aztec god Quetzalcoatl.

Although *Almanac of the Dead* is complex and encyclopedic, Silko is best known for her first novel *Ceremony.* Similar to *House Made of Dawn, Ceremony* tells the story of Tayo, a man of Native American descent recently returned from service in World War II. Tayo returns with feelings of guilt about the death of his cousin who served with him in the war, as well as about his uncle's death, which occurred while he was away. The novel's treatment of circularity suggests that we are all participants in a larger cycle of life and death.

The Chinese American Tradition: Maxine Hong Kingston, Amy Tan

In the Chinese American tradition, works such as Helena Kuo's *I've Come a Long Way* (1942), Jade Snow Wong's *Fifth Chinese Daughter* (1945), and the collaborative autobiography *Daughter of Confucius* (1952) have established a literary tradition focused on the interrelationships among language, culture, and family.

Maxine Hong Kingston (b. 1940) is one of the founding voices and most substantial contributors to post–World War II Asian American fiction. Her works include *The Woman Warrior: Memoirs of a Girlhood Among Ghosts* (1976), *China Men* (1980), *Tripmaster Monkey: His Fake Book* (1988), *Hawai'i One Summer* (1987), and, most recently, *The Fifth Book of Peace* (2003). Kingston herself was born in Sacramento, California, and attended college at the University of California, Berkeley. Much of her work consists of reworking traditional Chinese myths in order to examine their contemporary relevance. At the same time, she frequently uses these myths to put contemporary relationships and events in the context of cultural rather than chronological history. In *China Men* Kingston focuses her attention on the mythology surrounding the movement of several generations of Chinese men to America and back, beginning in the 1840s.

In *The Woman Warrior,* her most widely read novel, Kingston portrays the events of contemporary life according to ancient Chinese myths, although the present is never seen as merely replaying the past. Her best characters have strength, wisdom, and dignity. In one section of the novel, "No Name Woman," Kingston demonstrates how her mother used stories from Mainland China to try to control her daughter's behavior in America. The persistence of watchful ghosts and of ancestral memories in general is meant to guide behavior in a culture that has been transplanted to America. As Kinston's mother explains how, in China, watchful neighbors once destroyed the family's home because an aunt brought bad luck to the entire village, Kingston realizes that she, too, is haunted by the memory of an aunt she has never known. Both she and her aunt are dangerous because they are willing to violate traditional Chinese customs and go against their elders' wishes.

Kingston's most recent work, *The Fifth Book of Peace* (2003), operates on many levels and incorporates many different genres. It is at once a memoir of the burning of her Oakland home and the manuscript for *The Fourth Book of Peace* contained within it, a survey of Chinese myths surrounding the concept of peace, a recreation of her lost book, and a call to veterans of all wars to produce a body of writing that will speak out against war from the vantage point of experience.

Commenting on the fairly recent success of Kingston, Tan, and others, one British critic has declared that Chinese women in America seem to have won the universal rights to describing and defining the mother-daughter relationship. Amy Tan (b. 1952) is the author of *The Joy Luck Club* (1989), *The Kitchen God's Wife* (1991), *The Hundred*

❧ "COME ALL YE ASIAN AMERICAN WRITERS ❧ OF THE REAL AND THE FAKE"

Not all Asian Americans support the work of writers such as Amy Tan and Maxine Hong Kingston. Frank Chin (b. 1940), for example, rails against these writers for what he perceives to be their betrayal of authentic Chinese culture. Chin claims that Tan, and especially Kingston, have betrayed their origins and their culture in order to achieve success in America. In his notable 1991 article, "Come All Ye Asian American Writers of the Real and the Fake," Chin writes:

> *What seems to hold Asian American literature together is the popularity among whites of Maxine Hong Kingston's The Woman Warrior. . . ; David Henry Hwang's F.O.B. . . . and M. Butterfly. . . ; and Amy Tan's The Joy Luck Club. These works are held up before us as icons of our pride, symbols of our freedom from the icky gooey evil of . . . Chinese culture.*

In his opposition to Kingston in particular, Chin has helped bring attention to a strong division among Chinese writers and critics about artistic freedom, sexual politics, and the uses and appropriation of culture. In particular, Chin argues that the success of female Asian writers has been achieved at the expense of Asian men, who remain largely invisible. These current questions regarding the responsibility minority writers have to the culture with which they are identified echoes similar debates earlier in the twentieth century, especially among African American and Jewish American writers.

Secret Senses (1998), and *The Bonesetter's Daughter* (2001), as well as a number of children's books and nonfiction essays. Her first novel, *The Joy Luck Club,* is the story of four Chinese women who begin meeting to play mahjong, an ancient Chinese game. All recent immigrants to San Francisco, the women choose to work toward building a community of love and mutual caring, rather than to lapse into depression or give in to fear. They call themselves the Joy Luck Club. During their meetings the women tell stories about their families back in China and about the difficulties they experience in forging new ties in America.

More recently, Tan's fourth novel, *The Bonesetter's Daughter,* tells the story of LuLing Young and her daughter Ruth. Ruth has just come into possession of two texts written by her mother, who has just been diagnosed with Alzheimer's disease. The first is called "Things I Know Are True"; the second, "Things I Must Not Forget." LuLing has decided to trace her life and that of her family beginning with her birth in China in 1916; in doing so, she comes to understand and respect her own mother's journey to America and the choices she made once here.

Crossing the Borderlands of Fiction: Sandra Cisneros, Julia Alvarez, Gloria Anzaldua

The House on Mango Street (1984) by Sandra Cisneros (b. 1954) is one of the most popular and beloved collections of fiction to emerge from the 1980s. In it a series of short sketches describe Esperanza Cordero's coming-of-age in a new house in a Chicago neighborhood. Most of the stories describe the interrelationships among her family, the other children in the neighborhood, and her secret life of dreams. Esperanza has a wildly imaginative inner life that we sense will one day allow her to realize her dream of becoming a writer and escaping Mango Street. At the same time, it seems clear that she will one day return to help children in the old neighborhood.

In 2002, Cisneros released *Caramelo,* her long-awaited follow-up to *The House on Mango Street*. A much longer and more populated novel, much of it is about the nature of movement itself. We see this largely in the context of the multigenerational Reyes family and their travels from Mexico City to the United States and back again. By the end of the novel, we see that the universe and all of humanity is an interwoven cloth, much like Ceyala Reyes's grandmother's *caramelo rebozo,* or striped scarf.

The novels of Julia Alvarez (b. 1950), like those of Sandra Cisneros, interweave the stories of families over generations. Although she was born in New York in 1950, Julia Alvarez spent the majority of her childhood in the Dominican Republic. After her father's participation in a failed attempt to overthrow Trujillo, the nation's dictator, the family returned to the United States in 1960. Some of these autobiographical details are incorporated into her fiction. In the short stories comprising *How the Garcia Girls Lost Their Accents* (1991), for example, the Garcia family relocates to the United States under circumstances similar to those Alvarez herself experienced. Another of her works, *In the Time of the Butterflies* (1994), uses fictional elements to tell the true story of three sisters who were murdered for participating in an underground plot to overthrow the Trujillo government.

Sandra Cisneros

As the daughter of a Mexican father and Chicana (Mexican American) mother, and the only girl in a family of seven children, Sandra Cisneros has created prose and poetry works that reflect her childhood experiences and ethnic heritage. Cisneros's literary voice is found in that of her immediate family and that of her Latino community, making her characters very different from the characters of her American audience. In addition to a feminist's voice, she brings to her writing feelings of homelessness and displacement, a sense of divided cultural loyalties, feelings of alienation, and a sense of the degradation associated with poverty.

❧ ESPERANZA CORDERO AND ❧
THE HOUSE ON MANGO STREET

In one commonly anthologized chapter of **The House on Mango Street** *called "The Monkey Garden," Cisneros tries to capture the moment at which a young girl (Esperanza Cordero) laments her impending loss of innocence. She and the neighborhood children play in a nearby garden recently evacuated by a caged monkey. The garden holds innumerable wonders and becomes an active site for fantasy and imagination.*

Somebody started the lie that the monkey garden had been there before anything. We liked to think the garden could hide things for a thousand years. There beneath the roots of soggy flowers were the bones of murdered pirates and dinosaurs, the eye of a unicorn turned to coal.

Esperanza unknowingly uses the garden's landscape to work though all of her problems. One day everything changes as her friend Sally plays a game with some local boys. They steal her keys and make her kiss them in order to get the keys back. She willingly complies. The narrator cannot shake the impending sense of danger she feels not simply with the game but also with Sally's enjoyment of it. She has never felt more completely alienated, as though it is she who is missing the key to adulthood and understanding.

I looked at my feet in their white socks and ugly round shoes. They seemed far away. They didn't seem to be my feet anymore. And the garden that had been such a nice place to play didn't seem mine either.

————

Finally, *Yo!* (1997) finds one of the Garcia sisters returning to the Dominican Republic to reconnect with her childhood and with her cultural roots in a country that has become foreign to her.

Alvarez's fiction deals largely with the formation of individual identity and voice amidst pressures that are both generational and cultural. "Daughter of Invention," a story taken from *How the Garcia Girls Lost Their Accents,* beautifully captures the sacrifices parents are willing to make for their children even as they are consumed by pressures of which their children are unaware. Eventually, Yoyo (the most rebellious of the Garcia daughters) comes to understand that her mother has, in fact, secretly bestowed on her the power of invention and the ability to succeed in America.

If Julia Alvarez's fiction largely explores the difficulty in adjusting to life in America, much of Gloria Anzaldua's (1942–2004) work, by contrast, is focused on justifying the value of difference. Anzaldua died at age 61, just weeks away from earning her doctoral degree. During her life she was an activist, poet, essayist, and professor, whose book *Borderlands/La Frontera: The New Mestiza* (1987) has had an enormous influence on the way that various English, Spanish, and Chicano dialects are understood by non–Spanish-speaking Americans.

Anzaldua is unapologetic about her various uses and combinations of linguistic forms. She often shifts between languages in a single sentence, refusing to translate into a single privileged language. In "How to Tame a Wild Tongue," one of the essays in *Borderlands,* Anzaldua explains, "If you want to really hurt me, talk badly about my language. Ethnic identity is twin skin to linguistic identity–I am my language. Until I can take pride in my language, I cannot take pride in myself." Just because Anzaldua knows how to be hurt does not mean that she allows it to happen. Her ability to candidly describe the power and limitations of various approaches to mixed-language modes of expression is one way to ensure her own survival.

The Postcolonial Tradition: Jhumpa Lahiri

POSTCOLONIALISM refers to the rapid changes undergone by many countries following their liberation from European nations in the middle of the twentieth century. Most of these countries are located in Asia, Africa, and the Caribbean Ocean. With the removal of restrictions by the parent countries, these newly independent nations have struggled to recover economically and politically, and to achieve a relative stability previously forced on them. Along with these challenges, these once-colonial nations find themselves able to explore and reclaim their lost language, culture, and tradition. In many countries, these features of everyday life were officially restricted or outlawed. Major world figures in postcolonial literature include Salman Rushdie of India, 2001 Nobel Prize winner V.S. Naipaul who writes from Trinidad, Ngugi from the African nation of Kenya, and Bharati Mukherjee who was born in India and currently resides in the United States.

The desire for postcolonial writers to achieve popular literary recognition in America was greatly assisted by Jhumpa Lahiri's (b. 1967)

❧ "To Live in the Borderlands ❧ Means You . . ."

Gloria Anzaldua's notion of the "borderlands" refers to any number of encounters between cultures, ranging from the literal border between the United States and Mexico, to the spiritual differences between regional families. The MESTIZA, according to Anzaldua, is anyone who is caught between two oppositional languages or cultures. Her essays and poems in Borderlands/La Frontera *provide a number of attempts to empower the mestiza. In it she writes,*

> *The actual physical borderland that I'm dealing with in this book is the Texas–U.S., Southwest/Mexican border. The psychological borderlands, the sexual borderlands, and spiritual borderlands are not particular to the Southwest. In fact the Borderlands are physically present wherever two or more cultures edge each other, where people of different races occupy the same territory, where under, lower, middle and upper classes touch, where the space between two individuals shrinks with intimacy.*

One of Gloria Anzaldua's most powerful descriptions of the mestiza comes at the end of the poem "To Live in the Borderlands Means You. . . ." After describing some of the various ways in which Chicano immigrants have encountered and dealt with racist and prejudiced attitudes from both sides, she finally declares, "To survive in the Borderlands / you must live sin fronteras [without borders] / be a crossroads." In other words, one's cultural survival often depends on one's ability to resist rigid classification, to continually strive to increase rather than decrease one's means for personal expression.

---

winning of the 2000 Pulizer Prize for fiction. Unlike many other previous writers to achieve similar recognition, Lahiri's collection of short stories deals substantially with both Indian and Indian American culture. Roughly a third of the stories in the collection take place in India and are told from the perspective of Indian characters. In this light, the recognition of her work as an "American achievement" suggests that the definition of what constitutes American culture is undergoing a significant change.

The title story from *Interpreter of Maladies* (1999) perfectly exemplifies the many complications that can arise when we try to define ethnic writing. Although her family is of Indian descent, Lahiri herself was born in London and raised in Rhode Island. Her story involves an Indian American family touring the grounds of an ancient temple in India. The story is told from the perspective of an Indian tour guide who has never traveled outside of his native country.

Interpreter of Maladies describes Mr. Kapasi, a weekend tour guide who otherwise works as an interpreter for a local doctor. Raj and Mina Das and their three children, Ronny, Bobby, and Tina, have come to India to visit their relatives and have hired Mr. Kapasi to drive them out to the site of some ancient ruins depicting an enormous chariot drawn by a team of seven horses. As Mina discovers Mr. Kapasi's occupation as an interpreter, she compliments him on his privileged position. He has the power to determine the fate of lives. Later, when Mina and Mr. Kapasi are alone, she confesses her need of an interpreter. He responds by saying, "We do not face a language barrier. What need is there for an interpreter?" In this instance she is hoping that Mr. Kapasi can assess her problem, or malady, and provide some solution just as he translates the maladies of the patients who visit the doctor for whom he works. At the same time Mr. Kapasi finds in Mina an exoticism that in America might otherwise be commonplace. With respect to the status of ethnic literature, Lahiri's story explores the manifestation of difference itself, and its probing, persistent hunger to confront and destroy what it does not understand.

6. THE POSTMODERN MOMENT

Most critics in the field of literature agree that postmodernism is simply a convenient term for a manner of written expression that started to become popular in the early 1950s. Others see postmodernism as the logical extension of earlier modern thought. Perhaps the best way to begin describing postmodernism is to explain its relationship to modernism, a term that most commonly refers to post–World War I artistic expression.

Postmodern texts tend to portray the same feelings of alienation and fragmentation seen in modernism. Unlike modern works of fiction, postmodern works most often resist the urge to make a coherent whole out of the pieces. Instead, they accept the essential INDETERMINACY of certain aspects of existence. In Thomas Pynchon's (b. 1937) *V.* (1963), for example, Herbert Stencil fails to reconstruct the enigmatic and fractured history of a woman called V.; instead he discovers that such attempts to plot her transformation from a living woman to a collection of human and artificial pieces actually contribute to her further deformity. Postmodern writers react differently to these beliefs—some seem to lament the loss of structure, while others celebrate the freedom from conventional form.

There are several possible causes for the development of postmodern writing. One group of critics point to World War II and the various atrocities produced by it as likely triggers for the change in expression. They believe that the rapid rise of technology, the use of the atomic bomb, and the death machinery of the Holocaust qualitatively altered the way we experience the world. They understand the development of such technologies to indicate an essential unraveling of many of the historical narratives and bedrock principles on which earlier genres and texts were based.

Others see postmodernism as the inevitable result of capitalism. French social theorist Jean Baudrillard (b. 1929), for example, famously argues that the proliferation of duplications has produced a culture in which there are no longer any originals. Those who accept this theory believe that the world has changed as a result of two interrelated forces: modernization's effect on employment, labor, and the specialization of workforces; and the nature of advertising, the media, and the mass marketing of ideas. Postmodern texts often depict these changes.

One general feature of postmodern writing is that it tends not to distinguish between various kinds of art or different modes of

🖎 THE STRUCTURE OF SCIENTIFIC REVOLUTIONS 🖎

First published in 1962, Thomas Kuhn's (1922–1996) The Structure of Scientific Revolutions *challenges the idea that science is objective and that a fact is merely a fact. As Kuhn himself puts it, "Communication across the revolutionary divide is inevitably partial." Kuhn popularized the term* PARADIGM SHIFT *to describe the process by which the scientific community deals with revolutionary ideas that alter its existing beliefs.*

According to Kuhn, knowledge tends to become conventionalized through a threefold process. First, everyday science runs into an anomaly or piece of information it does not understand. It then enters a period of crisis in which scientists in the community are reluctant to accept the new piece of information as valid, in part because it threatens to overturn their existing way of thinking. Finally, the overwhelming power of the evidence becomes substantial enough to lead to a rapid and total shift in the community's approach to the particular topic.

Kuhn's theories are considered postmodern because they deny a clear and direct center from which to observe and make sense of the universe. As Kuhn explains, "An apparent arbitrary element . . . is always a formative ingredient of the beliefs espoused by a given scientific community at a given time." Like many postmodern writers of fiction, Kuhn assumes that meaning is constantly slipping. By extension, then, one can never definitively prove something true; one can only demonstrate that something is false. Linking ideas about science to postmodern literature and philosophy demonstrate that science and literature share a set of common concerns.

---

expression. A postmodern novel, such as Ishmael Reed's (b. 1938) *Mumbo Jumbo* (1972), for example, [Sidebar 6–1 The Structure of Scientificc Revolutions, pg 71] incorporates photographs and illustrations, as well as historical documents, footnotes, and bibliographies in order to parody the documentary style that American realists tend to take quite seriously. One consequence of this trend is that all aspects of daily life are able to be treated with equal consideration. In other words, if examples of postmodern art can be found in our everyday lives, does this mean that the artist is merely another agent of the postmodern world he is trying to critique? For this reason it is often difficult to distinguish between postmodernism as a literary movement and postmodernism as a way of looking at the world.

If Western philosophical thought is typically aimed at arriving at universal or categorical truths that can then be applied in all situations, postmodernism suggests that in fact there can only be relative truths. Postmodern theorists argue that there can be no single true story or authoritative viewpoint from which to order our lives—no METANARRATIVE to provide a means to realize our shared ideals. As many critics of postmodernism point out, the inherent danger of this way of thinking is that no individual actions or beliefs can be considered right or wrong. This MORAL RELATIVISM is perhaps the single greatest objection most philosophers and cultural thinkers have to postmodernism. If we are free to break away from the predominant, normalizing cultural myths, and if we recognize that the stories they tell are popular but not necessarily true, how do we then justify punishing individuals for having ideas and beliefs that differ from our own? As one character in Kurt Vonnegut's (b. 1922) *Slaughterhouse-Five* (1969) declares, "My God—he [a famous author] writes about Earthlings all the time, and they're all Americans. Practically nobody on Earth is an American."

Postmodern Exhaustion

John Barth (b. 1930) is an academic postmodernist whose work does a good job of illustrating the character of postmodernism. Barth's fiction—ranging from the mock historical epic *The Sot-Weed Factor,* to the speculative university-as-universe *Giles Goat Boy,* to the imaginative and metafictional retelling of three classic myths, *Chimer*—has explored a wide array of topics.

Barth has also written two important essays, the first of which is called "The Literature of Exhaustion" (1967). In it, Barth claims that existing modes and methods of representation are all "used up." He argues that overuse without invention or contribution has depleted most novelistic conventions of their usefulness. Most critics read Barth's essay as a declaration of "the death of the novel," meaning that the genre as we know it would soon cease to be a viable means for an artist to present his or her material.

In a second essay, "The Literature of Replenishment," which was published in 1979, Barth insisted that his first essay had been misunderstood. He was not signaling the death of the novel. Instead, Barth claims, he was merely describing the end of a stage in the history of intellectual thought. Together, Barth insists, both essays point to some of the possible directions in which new fiction might go.

❧ PLAY ❧

Beginning with Homo Ludens (1938), a philosophical work by Johan Huizinga (1872–1945), the idea of "play" has had a significant influence on contemporary thought and the idea of literature itself. Huizinga proposed that play is one of the fundamental aspects of human life, even going so far as to suggest that it might precede other, more rational structures we normally associate with culture. If cultural institutions are oppress or otherwise contrain certain individuals within them, play might be considered liberating because it undermines some of the assumptions upon which those institutions are built. Works by James Joyce (1882–1941), Vladimir Nabokov (1899– 1977), Thomas Pynchon, and particularly Donald Barthelme (1931– 1989) are often characterized by the prevalence of their word play. Barthelme's Snow White *(1972) mocks conventional fairy tale language in order to overturn the oppressive gender expectations and morals common to the genre.*

Critics who discuss gay and lesbian themes in literature have also adopted the idea of play to argue that there is nothing fundamental or essential about gender. This means that men and women are taught to behave in certain ways simply because they happen to belong to a particular culture. These theorists often talk about "performance" as one way for an individual to break out of his or her predetermined role. By performing different roles, they claim, men and women of all different sexual orientations can assert their freedom to think and act as they choose.

Kurt Vonnegut: "Rarefied, Luminous Spaghetti" Drawn with Adult Crayons

Kurt Vonnegut is the celebrated author of numerous novels, short story collections, and essays. Perhaps more than any other contemporary writer, Vonnegut exhibits a sense of genuine humanity without lapsing into sentimentality. His works are at once simple to read and complex to absorb. In his most famous work, *Slaughterhouse-Five* (1969), Vonnegut uses the Tramalfadorians, a race of aliens, as a way to try to make sense of his captivity during World War II in the German city of Dresden. Vonnegut makes use of Tramalfadorian theories of time and free will in order to rationalize an otherwise irrational

❧ THIS IS NOT A PIPE ❧

Rene Magritte's (1898–1967) famous painting "Ceçi n'est pas une pipe" (1926) depicts a realistic looking pipe along with the above caption, which translates from the French to "This is not a pipe." Magritte is suggesting that many contemporary thinkers confuse the image of an object with the thing itself. One should not mistake form for content.

Michel Foucault (1926–1984), a highly influential French theorist, wrote a book about Magritte's work in which he compared the painting to some of the tenets of postmodern language theory. Foucault argued that writers, too, often confuse the word for the essence it is meant to describe. Postmodernism writers, Foucault argued, also want their audiences to recognize that words don't have essential meanings. Instead, every word is defined by its relationship to other words.

Magritte's painting is a significant artistic forerunner to a number of postmodern writers that self-consciously manipulate structure as part of their work. John Barth, for one, commonly uses the materials and structures of historical writing in order to undermine the authority that they are too often thought to carry with them. In The Sot-Weed Factor (1960), Barth incorporates an actual satirical poem by a minor poet of the eighteenth century, Ebenezer Cook (1670–1732), so that he might then scrutinize it alongside his own highly satirical linguistic invention.

---

response to the horrors of war. In one celebrated passage, Vonnegut imagines a bombing attack like Dresden in reverse. In this way he offers a hopeful retelling of the possibilities of human collectivity when it is directed toward peace as opposed to hate.

Slaughterhouse-Five shows that, as humans, peace is our greatest desire, while war seems to be our favorite pastime. One character highlights the absurdity of writing against war by asking, "Why don't you write an anti-*glacier* book instead?" the suggestion being that wars are as inevitable and implacable as moving mountains of ice. *Slaughterhouse-Five* goes on to tell the story of Billy Pilgrim, a war veteran who has "become unstuck in time," so that he jumps from place to place throughout the chronology of his life. Additionally, Billy believes that in 1967 he was abducted by a flying saucer

Kurt Vonnegut

A self-proclaimed humanist and socialist, Vonnegut is known for his imaginative and satirical science fiction works, which are based on human nature. He often writes on the chaotic, irrational violence and alienation of modern life. He attributes his unembellished writing style to his work as a reporter in his early years. Vonnegut is best known as the author of the semi-autobiographical *Slaughterhouse-Five* (1969), a novel about an American soldier who is captured by German soldiers and who becomes "unstuck in time." He visits random periods of his life, to be captured later on by aliens and taken to the planet Tramalfadore. His antiauthoritarian themes continue to attract the American audience.

from the planet Tramalfadore and kept naked in a zoo where he was mated with a former Hollywood movie star named Montana Wild-hack. He believes the two phenomena to be unrelated. Throughout the novel, Billy moves from scene to scene, seemingly at random. This apparent randomness echoes the same sort of chaos Billy encountered in the war.

Included in *Slaughterhouse-Five* is a description of Tramalfadorian books that might also serve as the best commentary on Vonnnegut's own fiction:

> Each clump of symbols is a brief, urgent message—escribing a situation, a scene. We Tramalfadorians read them all at once, not one after the other. There isn't any particular relationship between all the messages, except that the author has chosen them carefully, so that, when seen all at once, they produce an image of life that is beautiful and surprising and deep. There is no beginning, no middle, no end, no suspense, no moral, no causes, no effects.

Not only is Vonnegut a master of integrating multiple genres and media into a single, surprisingly coherent commentary on the modern condition, he is also a master at taking them apart again. In *Breakfast of Champions* (1973), used car salesman Dwayne Hoover meets Kilgore Trout, a hack science fiction writer who appears in many of Vonnegut's novels and is a likely alter-ego for the author. At the close of the novel, Hoover meets Vonnegut himself. Vonnegut uses this layering of character and author to question whether his characters' lives are the product of societal forces or of his own psychological influence as author. Seen as the culmination of Vonnegut's earlier work, *Breakfast of Champions* uses childlike prose to discuss the conventions, limitations, and possibilities of the novel's form and the relationship between any author and the fictive worlds he or she creates.

Thomas Pynchon: Exploring the Excluded Middle

There is little doubt that Thomas Pynchon (b. 1937) is one of the most complex and challenging writers to emerge from the 1960s. If one of the qualities of the postmodern character is that he or she has no center and can play many roles at once, Thomas Pynchon's own status as an author has served as an apt comment on this phenomenon. Pynchon studied nuclear engineering at Cornell University, spent some time in the Navy, and later went to work as a technical writer for Boeing in Seattle. Pynchon completed his first novel, *V.,* in Mexico City in 1963. Beyond that, very little about Pynchon is known. But Pynchon is not a recluse in the traditional sense. One could argue that Pynchon's anticelebrity is itself a form of celebrity.

Pynchon is the author of five novels: *V.* (1963), *The Crying of Lot 49* (1966), *Gravity's Rainbow* (1973), *Vineland* (1989), and *Mason & Dixon* (1997). Together, they describe a world that is made up of complex networks of power and communication that are at once intensely mechanistic and surprisingly human. In nearly all his works, Pynchon's characters become immersed in multinational conspiracies that ignore national boundaries. Global alliances and networks are the norm and not the exception. While often subversive, these collectivities are not necessarily sinister, or even unethical. Pynchon can capture the modern tendency toward "nihilism," or the absence of knowledge, truth and purpose, like no other writer in America today.

The Crying of Lot 49, Pynchon's most accessible novel, also happens to be the one most self-consciously concerned with the postmodern condition. The novel opens with Oedipa Maas's discovery that she has been named executor of her late boyfriend Pierce Inverarity's multimillion dollar estate. While exploring his holdings, she stumbles upon what she believes to be an underground information network called the Trystero. No one is really certain exactly what the Trystero is or who controls it. As Oedipa travels deeper and deeper into the mystery, she ends up believing in the existence of an enormous underground conspiracy that keeps much of the unknown world in constant contact. Even so, the Trystero seems to be all structure and no content as nothing ever happens as a result of the organization's clandestine operations. If anything, the Trystero comes to represent the literal and metaphorical counterforce to mainstream America. It is something like the complete and unified vision of all the sixties counterculture movements taken as a whole. *The Crying of Lot 49* finally seems to say that metaphors do not merely describe reality, they also have the power to create it.

Gravity's Rainbow is Pynchon's masterpiece. It is also one of the most complex and challenging novels of the American century. It features no fewer than a dozen major plotlines and over 400 characters. In it ANTIHERO Tyrone Slothrop, an American soldier stationed in London during World War II, discovers that the mapped locations of his sexual exploits coincide nearly perfectly with the impact sites made by German V-2 rockets. It turns out that as an infant Slothrop was the subject of a rather strange Pavlovian experiment that was never actually completed. This discovery sets him on a quest all across Europe to make sense of his origins and to reveal the numerous agencies and corporations that have an interest in him. At the heart of his quest is the mysterious Rocket 00000. The novel warns against the rise of transnational corporations, particularly because of their lack of allegiance to their nation of origin in times of war.

Raymond Carver: The Depth of Surface

Raymond Carver (1938–1988) is the author of several collections of short stories, the most impressive of which are *What We Talk About When We Talk About Love* (1981) and *Cathedral* (1983). In them, he perfected a style of writing Tom Wolfe referred to as "K-mart realism." Wolfe uses the term to describe hyperdetailed presentations of everyday situations. Carver is also what is referred to as a minimalist. MINIMALISM is a movement in many different artistic areas that began in the 1960s. Minimalists use the most basic designs, structures, and language, and they tend to make as invisible as possible the artist's own individuality. In literature, this approach has made Raymond Carver a master of surface. His characters coexist with objects so intimately that the two sometimes become indistinguishable from one another, as when a recently divorced man is viewed alongside his possessions, which are strewn across the front lawn.

Very often, Carver's stories explore a shared anticipation for very slight changes in circumstance, or small turns of attention and focus. Paradoxically, their eventual outcomes achieve a certain weight precisely because they are minute and detailed. His stories are often set in mundane locations like the supermarket, the shopping mall, or a garage sale. Carver's characters also tend to be lower or middle class with few instantly impressive characteristics. Their lives rest on the hinge of revelation, and their silences reveal more than most people's conversations. Oftentimes, Carver's characters have something to hide that nevertheless becomes exposed against their will.

In "Cathedral," Carver's most celebrated short story, the narrator is reluctant to have a blind man named Robert visit his wife at their home. Later that night, seated before the television, the narrator finds himself unable to describe a cathedral. Robert suggests that he draw one on heavy paper so that the blind man might be able to trace his fingers along the blueprint and feel the materiality of the image. In a remarkable reversal, however, it is Robert who guides the narrator. As he closes his eyes, he achieves the sensation of being inside nothing at all. This feeling of both omnipresence and emptiness is one of the culminating effects of Carver's multilayered exploration of the interaction between human experience and the material world.

Don DeLillo: Connecting the Dots

Don DeLillo (b. 1936) began his career in advertising. In his early novel *Americana* (1971) DeLillo argues that advertising has created the image of the contemporary person—and that this person is but an image.

> In this country there is a universal third person, a man we all want to be. Advertising has discovered this man. It uses him to express the possibilities open to the consumer. To consume in America is not to buy; it is to dream. Advertising is the suggestion that the dream of entering the third person singular might possibly be fulfilled.

Pervading Don DeLillo's fiction is the sense of the conspiratorial underpinnings of everyday life and the possibility of finding fulfillment within such hidden, prescribed systems.

DeLillo is the author of more than a dozen novels, the most successful of which are *White Noise* (1984) and *Underworld* (1997). He is fascinated with the commonplace, the everyday, especially in the locations he chooses to depict, and the reverence his characters seem to have for them. In *White Noise,* for example, Murray's religious reverence for the supermarket elevates the everyday to the level of a postmodern temple. In these settings, his characters are often in search of a hidden word, a special name, or a recovered memory that will turn the ordinary into some secularized miracle of belonging, or else will grant a firmer, more justified, heightened rationale for one's own alienation.

Jargon is an important feature of DeLillo's style. Certain phrases circulate throughout his texts with the force and permanence of objects. In *White Noise* for example, an "airborne toxic event" (a dangerous chemical cloud that results from an industrial accident) becomes a way to describe a horrific happening that, on numerous repetitions, seems to take the place of the atrocity it is trying to mask. Thus, the world is reordered according to the language that is used to describe it, and language no longer has any relation to reality.

❧ THE MOST PHOTOGRAPHED BARN IN AMERICA ❧

Following is a perfect example of what happens when a postmodern sensibility is brought to bear on a scene from everyday life. The dialogue takes place near the beginning of Don DeLillo's White Noise. *Jack Gladney and his colleague Murray Siskind have just traveled to Farmington to visit "the most photographed barn in America."*

No one sees the barn. . . . Once you've seen the signs about the barn, it becomes impossible to see the barn. . . . We're not here to capture an image, we're here to maintain one. Every photograph reinforces the aura. Can you feel it, Jack? An accumulation of nameless energies. . . . Being here is a kind of spiritual surrender. We see only what the others see. The thousands who were here in the past, those who will come in the future. We've agreed to be part of a collective perception. This literally colors our vision. A religious experience in a way, like all tourism. . . . They are taking pictures of taking pictures. . . . What was the barn like before it was photographed. . .? What did it look like, how was it different from other barns, how was it similar to other barns? We can't answer these questions because we've read the signs, seen the people snapping the pictures. We can't get outside the aura. We're part of the aura. We're here, we're now.

The material barn, Murray argues, has become less responsible for its own meaning than all of the image manipulation, enhancement, and framing, that has sprung up around it; in light of the numerous photographs and other reproductions of scene, the object itself has all but disappeared.

Cormac McCarthy: The Universal Democracy of Violence

Cormac McCarthy (b. 1933) is the author of eight novels, many of which examine the themes of the classic western novel and the mythologies of the Old West itself. While McCarthy's "border trilogy"—consisting of *All the Pretty Horses* (1992), *The Crossing* (1994), and *Cities of the Plain* (1998)—has enjoyed more popularity than *Blood Meridian* (1985), the latter is the most important of McCarthy's novels. In it, the nameless narrator referred to only as "the kid" joins a band of men who are hired to scalp Indians along the Texas–Mexico border beginning in 1849.

Blood Meridian is a complicated novel because of its relationship to the historical western novel. At times, *Blood Meridian* seems to endorse many of the predominant mythologies of the Old West; at others it completely subverts, or undermines, them. Complicating this question is the novel's most central figure, Judge Holden, an incredible rhetorician who endorses the ideas of modernism at the same time that he uses postmodern ideas and arguments to demonstrate how his own logic will lead to disaster. Holden seemingly guides the kid toward an apocalyptic confrontation with himself. Against the outcome of their relationship, *Blood Meridian* treats violence among the Americans, the Mexicans, and the Indians as identical, and in this way McCarthy's novel resists favoring any one group over the others.

In a scene crucial to the novel's postmodern ethic, the men in the war party become victims of snow blindness and are forced to conceive of a new relationship between the land and the creatures on it, where all "were bequeathed a strange equality."

In the neuter austerity of that terrain all phenomena were bequeathed a strange equality and not one thing nor spider nor stone nor blade of grass could put forth claim to precedence. The very clarity of these articles belied their familiarity, for the eye predicates the whole on some feature or part and here was nothing more luminous than another and nothing more enshadowed and in the optical democracy of such landscapes all preference is made whimsical and a man and a rock become endowed with unguessed kinships.

This approach to the world can have one of two effects: It can support the sort of brutal mindless violence seen throughout the novel, or it can point to an ethical system in which all living things are considered equally valuable *because* nothing has priority over anything else.

Where Will We Have Gone From Here?

It is impossible to predict the future of American literature—what might define its fears, or where its hope might lie. One of the virtues of the writers in this chapter, and of the postmodernists more generally, is that they are largely resistant to tradition. For this reason, they tend to write about a wider variety of topics from a broader range of perspectives, leaving the breadth and depth of their fiction to reflect the limits of the known and imagined universes, as well as the mirrored surfaces where they intersect.

TIMELINE

Science, Technology, and the Arts	Literature	History
1945 U.S. explodes first atomic bomb		End of World War II
1946		The United Nations is founded
1947	Warren *All the King's Men*	The "Truman Doctrine"
1948 The term *Cold War* becomes widely used		The first of McCarthy's "witch hunts"
1949 Volkswagen Beetle sold in America	Mailer *The Naked and the Dead*	Berlin Airlift
1950	Miller *Death of a Salesman*	
1951 Univac I becomes the first mass-produced computer		The Korean War begins
1952	Salinger *The Catcher in the Rye*	
	Arendt *The Origins of Totalitarianism*	
	O'Connor *Wise Blood*	
	Ellison *Invisible Man*	
	Steinbeck *East of Eden*	
1953 Watson and Crick discover the structure of DNA	Miller *The Crucible*	Eisenhower succeeds Truman
Kinsey's *Sexual Behavior of the Human Female*		Korean War ends
Transistor radio invented		
Hugh Heffner publishes *Playboy*		
1954 More than half of American homes have televisions		*Brown v. Board of Education*
Oral contraceptives invented		
1955 Rock n' Roll becomes popular	Nabokov *Lolita*	Rosa Parks refuses to sit at back of a bus
Film: *Rebel Without a Cause*		
1956 U.S. explodes first hydrogen bomb	Ginsberg "Howl"	
1957 *Sputnik* (Soviet) becomes first satellite launched into outer space	Kerouac *On the Road*	
1958 Heisenberg's Uncertainty Principle		
Laser invented		

1959	Bellow *Henderson the Rain King*	Alaska and Hawaii admitted as states
1960 Birth control pill invented	Updike *Rabbit Run*	Nixon-Kennedy debates
1961 Yuri Gagarin (Soviet) first astronaut	Barth *The Sot-Weed Factor*	
1962 Film: *The Manchurian Candidate*	Lee *To Kill a Mockingbird*	Kennedy succeeds Eisenhower
	Heller *Catch-22*	Cuban Missile Crisis
	Plath *The Bell Jar*	
	Kesey *One Flew over the Cuckoo's Nest*	
1963		President Kennedy assassinated
		Lyndon Johnson becomes President
	Pynchon *V.*	"Free Speech Movement"
1964 Smoking is proved dangerous		Gulf of Tonkin Resolution
1965 Hypertext invented, forerunner to the internet NutraSweet goes on the market	Bellow *Herzog*	Malcolm X assassinated
1966		Cultural Revolution in China
		Black Panther Party founded
1967		
	Capote *In Cold Blood*	Martin Luther King, Jr., assassinated
1968 RAM (random access memory) invented	Styron *The Confessions of Nat Turner*	
	Mailer *Armies of the Night*	Nixon succeeds Johnson
1969 Neil Armstrong becomes first man to walk on the Moon	Momaday *House Made of Dawn*	26th Amendment to Constitution, allowing 18-year-olds to vote, ratified
300,000 people attend Woodstock	Vonnegut *Slaughterhouse-Five*	
	Roth *Portnoy's Complaint*	
1970 First segments of "The Pentagon Papers" appear in *The New York Times*		U.S. invades Cambodia
1972		Nixon meets Mao
1973 U.S. launches Skylab space station		The U.S. withdraws from Vietnam
1974 Discovery of "Lucy" skeleton in Africa	Reed *Mumbo Jumbo*	President Nixon resigns
	Pynchon *Gravity's Rainbow*	Ford becomes President
		Telephone set up between the White House and the Kremlin
	Pirsig *Zen and the Art of Motorcycle Maintenance*	South Vietnam surrenders to North
1975 Bill Gates and Paul Allen found Microsoft		

1976 Viking II sends photos from Mars in color	Ashbery *Self Portrait in a Convex Mirror* Hong Kingston *The Woman Warrior*	
1977	Morrison *Song of Solomon* Silko *Ceremony*	Carter succeeds Ford
1978 First test-tube baby		
1979 Cellular phone invented		Three Mile Island suffers near meltdown
1980 Ted Turner launches CNN		U.S. boycotts Olympics in Moscow
1981 IBM releases its first PC First case of AIDS discovered	Carver *What We Talk about When We Talk About Love*	Reagan succeeds Ford
1982 AT&T monopoly broken up	Walker *The Color Purple*	
1983 CDs first go on sale	Carver *Cathedral*	Reagan increases military funding
1984 Ozone hole discovered over Antarctica "Baby Fae" receives baboon heart	DeLillo *White Noise* Didion *Democracy* Gibson *Neuromancer*	U.K. agrees to return Hong Kong to China Reagan visits China
1985 U.S.A. for Africa records "We Are the World"	McCarthy *Blood Meridian*	Reagan's second inauguration
1986 Fox becomes the fourth television network Space shuttle *Challenger* explodes	O'Brien *Nuclear Age* McMurtry's *Lonesome Dove* wins Pulitzer Prize	Iran-Contra Affair Reagan and Gorbachev sign INF treaty
1987	Morrison *Beloved*	
1988 Prozac invented	Wolfe *The Bonfire of the Vanities*	
1989 Viruses hit the Internet	Tan *The Joy Luck Club* Pynchon *Vineland*	Bush succeeds Reagan Fall of the Berlin Wall
1990 The Human Genome Project begins Hubble Telescope deployed	Updike *Rabbit at Rest*	
1991 Salman Rushdie makes an appearance in NY, defying death threats by Iran	Silko *Almanac of the Dead*	The Gulf War against Iraq
1992	Morrison *Jazz*	NAFTA formed Clinton succeeds Bush
1993 HTML becomes code for web design		
1994 Nearly one-third of U.S. homes equipped with a computer		

1995 U.S. scientist achieves lowest temperature ever recorded: 200 nanoKelvins

1996 30 million U.S. Internet users

1997 DVDs go on sale

1998 MP3s downloaded for free

1999 Viruses hit the Internet

2000 Y2K threatens the computer industry

2001 Microsoft introduces Windows XP

2002

2003 The Human Genome Project is completed
Severe acute respiratory syndrome (SARS) breaks out in Asia and Canada

2004 South Koreans clone human embryo to harvest stem cells for research

2005 Cancer becomes top killer in U.S.

Tan *The Hundred Secret Senses*

DeLillo *Underworld*
Pynchon *Mason & Dixon*
Roth *American Pastoral*
Morrison *Paradise*

Lahiri's *Interpreter of Maladies*

Tan *The Bonesetter's Daughter*

Cisneros *Caramelo*
Hong Kingston *The Fifth Book of Peace*

Robinson's *Gilead* wins Pulitzer Prize for fiction

Oklahoma City bombing
Troops sent to Bosnia

Welfare reform bill enacted

Monica Lewinsky scandal

U.S. population more than 280 million
Bush succeeds Clinton
World Trade Center and Pentagon attacked

U.S. and Britain invade Iraq
Space Shuttle *Columbia* explodes

U.S. returns sovereignty to Iraq (but maintains troop presence)

GLOSSARY OF TERMS

antihero a common feature of post-modern literature, referring to the protagonist of a work of fiction who lacks many or all of the admirable characteristics of a traditional hero. (See Yossarian in Joseph Heller's *Catch-22* or Tyrone Slothrop in Thomas Pynchon's *Gravity's Rainbow.*)

atomic age the period beginning with the United States's detonation of the first nuclear reaction on December 2, 1942. The Soviet Union quickly responded with testing of its own. The term refers to the influence of nuclear activity on the ideas and beliefs of everyone living under the threat of nuclear war.

avant-garde a term used to refer to the newest, most experimental, and least conventional movements at any given time, particularly in reference to the arts. *Avant-garde* is French for "vanguard," which refers to the troops at the head of an army.

Beat generation from the term *beat* as coined by Jack Kerouac to describe a state of cultural exhaustion but also one of elevated awareness. Beat writers included Allen Ginsberg, Neal Cassady, Gary Snyder, and William Burroughs.

Black Arts Movement artistic movement that gained the most influence from 1965 to 1974. Artists in the movement tended to portray black culture as powerful, beautiful, and as a significant contributor to western thought; the movement was related to Black Nationalism.

canon the current body of accepted or commonly taught literary works. The status of the canon is a source of constant political debate, particularly among writers, critics, and teachers who would like to see more representative work by women and writers of color.

Cold War the decades-long confrontation between the United States and the Soviet Union, beginning just after World War II. The Cold War was a war of ideologies, and both countries worked to gain political influence over the other country and technological supremacy relative to one another. It was called a "Cold War" because no battles were ever *directly* fought between the two sides.

communism economic theory in which the community as a whole owns and shares property, and a form of socialism in Marxist theory; the political system adopted by the Soviet Union, China, Cuba, North Korea, North Vietnam, and other nations who opposed the United States during the Cold War

confessional poetry type of poetry strongly associated with Robert Lowell. Confessional poems tend to focus on the life of the artist and often explore family themes.

conscientious objector an individual who refuses to take part in war as a result of his or her own individual conscience. Muhammad Ali was famously jailed for refusing to fight in the Vietnam War.

conspicuous consumption a term used by American economist Thorstein Veblen to describe a situation in which overconsumption had become the norm. Motivated by such social factors as keeping up with the neighbors, conspicuous consumption is often seen as an addiction arising from consumerism.

counterculture movement youth rebellion that opposes an existing mainstream culture or set of beliefs. The term is most commonly used to refer to the Youth Movement in the United States during the 1960s; the countercultural movement was characterized by lifestyle changes in music, clothing, drugs, employment, and spirituality.

Cuban Missile Crisis thirteen-day standoff between the United States and the Soviet Union. Under President Kennedy's orders, the U.S. Navy prevented the Soviets from bringing nuclear missiles to Cuba.

cultural revolution a movement led by Mao Tse-Tung in China that encouraged the Red Guard (mostly comprised of youths) to eliminate members of the middle class in order to create a classless society. Those killed were largely intellectuals and politicians.

deconstructionist a philosophy and method of analysis popularized by the work of French literary critic Jacques Derrida. Because of the uncertainty of language itself, deconstructionists argue that no text can have a fixed and/or coherent meaning.

domino theory theory made popular at the beginning of the Cold War which asserts that any nation becoming Communist will likely cause the nations around it to follow suit

epithet a descriptive word or phrase used to describe a person or thing

essentialism defining a group of people by one or a small set of properties

ethnicity term used to describe a population or group of people that share the same national origin, language, and history, or that have similar customs and beliefs

Existentialism philosophy made popular by French philosopher Jean Paul Sartre in the 20th century. Existentialists believe that existence precedes essence. That is, there exists no God-given or Platonic "essence" that determines who a person is, no meaning or purpose to life other than what an individual creates for himself or herself. A person exists and defines who or what he/she is through his or her life choices.

free verse unrhymed verse without a consistent metrical pattern; free verse poems may or may not rhyme and do not adhere to any conventional pattern. Robert Frost called free verse, "playing tennis without a net."

House Un-American Activities Committee (HUAC) standing committee of the House of Representatives that, in the 1950s, heard testimony engineered by Senator Joseph McCarthy and which was supposedly designed to determine the nature and extent of Communist influence in the U.S. government and major industries

imperialist a political system in which one nation rules or profoundly influences the choices of another nation; used to describe the policies of empires, such as the Roman or British empires and, by extension, nations with empire-like influence

indeterminacy a reference to those places in a text that cannot be interpreted or that resist a single meaning

Korean Conflict a war between Communist North Korea and Democratic South Korea lasting from 1950 to 1953 and ending in a cease fire. The United States intervened on behalf of South Korea, though it never officially declared war.

literary journalism an approach to reporting made popular in the 1950s and 1960s. The goal of literary journalists is to use the techniques of fiction in order to more accurately and forcefully capture the experience and impact of individuals, events, and/or cultural phenomena.

matrilineal a social system in which descent and inheritance are traced through the female line

McCarthyism accusing others of disloyalty or treason, while knowing that the accusations are false. The term comes from the name of Senator Joseph McCarthy who accused many Americans of being Communist sympathizers during the 1950s.

mestiza/o a person born of mixed parents, particularly someone with a combination of Spanish and American Indian blood. The term is most often used to refer to individuals in Latin America or the Southwest region of the United States.

metanarrative in literature, a style of writing or presentation in which the author (and sometimes his or her characters) indicate an awarness of and comment on their status as creators and participants in fictions

military-industrial complex a term of warning used by President Eisenhower to describe the growing cooperation between the United States economy and the military. Eisenhower feared that their alliance would promote military action and negatively affect economies around the world.

minimalism a movement that affected the visual and linguistic arts beginning in the 1960s; minimalists used only the most basic designs and forms. In writing, minimalists tried to make invisible their own presence in their work.

moral relativism refers to the belief that if all cultures are valid and different, and no meaning is fixed or certain, then there can be no absolutes, including good and evil

paradigm shift a term popularized by Thomas Kuhn and that refers to the process by which the scientific community is first resistant to and then accepts revolutionary ideas that alter its existing beliefs

poetry of witness term made popular by the work of Carolyn Forché. The term is used to describe the application to poetry of a social space that combines public and private interests.

populist a supporter of the rights and power of ordinary people

postethnic a movement that attempts to combine a strong awareness of rooted belonging with the freedom for any individual to affiliate temporarily with multiple ethnicities

postcolonialism an area of politics and philosophy concerned with understanding the social and psychological impact European nations have had on the individuals they have colonized. Studies in postcolonialism often focus on the forms of resistance used by the indigenous populations.

postmodern a recognized departure from the modernism of the 1920s. Postmodernists tend to use multiple styles and approaches in their writing, tend to argue against the possibility of fixed meanings, and often tamper with the conventions of narrative form.

red scare phenomenon in 1950s Cold War America referring to the fear that Communist agents had infiltrated the U.S. government or that Communist sympathizers were secretly controlling American business and media interests

self-conscious narrator a literary convention in which the narrator of a work of fiction calls attention to himself or herself and the artificiality of the fictional work

silent majority the group that Richard Nixon appealed to in his successful bid for the presidency. Nixon claimed to speak for the overwhelming majority of Americans who did not necessarily tend to protest or speak out on behalf of their beliefs.

space age the period beginning with the Soviet's launch of *Sputnik,* the first satellite into outer space on October 4, 1957. The United States responded by completely overhauling the aerospace industry as well as the military.

Vietnam War military conflict between North and South Vietnam lasting from 1957 to 1975. The United States intervened on the part of South Vietnam in order to prevent the spread of communism.

Watergate scandal involving a Republican-led break-in at the Democratic offices at the Watergate apartment complex, which led to the resignation of President Richard Nixon. In a series of articles appearing in the *Washington Post,* reporters Bob Woodward and Carl Bernstein broke the case.

BIOGRAPHICAL GLOSSARY

Ali, Muhammad (b. 1942) Born Cassius Clay, Jr., Ali changed his name after joining the Black Muslims in 1964. Ali won the heavyweight title of the world in boxing in 1964. Outside of sport, Ali was an incredibly articulate and charismatic individual who spoke candidly about his political and social beliefs. In 1967 Ali refused to be drafted and spent three and a half years in prison while his appeal for "conscientious observer" status made its way to the Supreme Court. The decision was overturned and Ali regained the right to box. Over his career, Ali would win the title an unprecedented three times. His match with George Foreman in Zaire was famously described by Norman Mailer in *The Fight* (1975).

Barth, John (b. 1930) Much of Barth's writing is centered around the Maryland shore where he grew up. John Barth is best known as an academic postmodernist whose work whose fiction explores a range of topics from the mock-historical epic *The Sot-Weed Factor* (1960), to the speculative university-as-universe *Giles Goat Boy* (1966), to the imaginative and meta-fictional retelling of three classic myths, *Chimera* (1972). The highly academic, postmodern quality of his writing is often criticized as much as it is admired for its creativity. Barth is also the author of two highly controversial essays that examine the status of American fiction: "The Literature of Exhaustion" (1967) and "The Literature of Replenishment" (1979).

Cage, John (1912–1992) John Cage was one of the most influential composers of the twentieth century. Cage experimented with electronic methods of composing long before the use of electronic synthesizers became common practice. His music was influenced by his exposure to Eastern philosophy. As a result of this exposure, Cage began to experiment with randomness and chance as compositional factors. Cage's avant-garde approach to the very definition of what constitutes music was highly influential, particularly in the 1960s. Cage's reputation endured until his death in 1992.

Didion, Joan (b. 1934) Didion was born in Sacramento and raised in California's central valley, an area of the state she often returns to in her work. Didion attended the University of California, Berkeley, until she moved to New York after winning a *Vogue* magazine essay contest and a job offer. Though Didion has published a number of novels, among them *Run River* (1963), *Play it as it Lays* (1970) *Democracy* (1984), and *The Last Thing He Wanted* (1996), her reputation rests largely on her non-fiction essays and frequent magazine contributions on the topic of politics. Of her essay collections, the most famous are *Slouching toward Bethlehem* (1968) and *The White Album* (1979). Didion is one of the most remarkable non-fiction prose writers in English.

Dylan, Bob (b. 1941) Born Robert Zimmerman. U.S. musician. Perhaps the greatest and most influential singer/songwriter of the twentieth century, Bob Dylan has been performing since the late 1950s. More than any other artist of his generation Dylan has both captured and defined the popular imagination. His most famous anti-war songs include "Blowin' in the Wind," "Masters of War," and "The Times They Are a Changin'." Dylan continued to grow as an artist and reached his creative peak with *Highway 61 Revisited* and *Blonde on Blonde*. In 2004, Dylan released *Chronicles,* the first volume of his autobiography. He has been nominated for the Nobel Prize in Literature several times.

Eisenhower, Dwight D. (1890–1969) Running under the famous slogan "I Like Ike," Eisenhower became the 34th president of the United States after serving as Commander of the Allied Forces in World War II. Eisenhower presided over much of the post-World War II boom in U.S. politics and economics. As a result, his administration was largely responsible for laying the foundation for the U.S. foreign policy in the decades to come, particularly with respect to the Soviet Union and the Cold War. Eisenhower was aware of the role he and the military had played in shaping the U.S. economy and even warned of it in his farewell address as President.

Holiday, Billie (1915–1959) Nicknamed "Lady Day," Holiday is regarded as the first jazz musician to connect with mainstream audiences. The strength of her personality revolutionized the art of pop vocals. While engaged in a series of chaotic and destructive relationships, Holiday recorded a number of heartfelt and moving songs, including "Strange Fruit" and "God Bless the Child." The former is an intense and moving examination of Southern racism and was banned by many radio stations.

Johnson, Lyndon (1908–1973) 36th president of the United States, Johnson was sworn in on the day of President Kennedy's assassination. He was then reelected to a second term in 1964. Johnson had hoped to oversee what he called the "Great Society," a series of groundbreaking civil rights laws and social welfare policies. These accomplishments have been overshadowed by Johnson's decision to intensify the U.S. involvement in the Vietnam War. Because of strong anti-war feeling in the U.S. Johnson opted not to run for a second term. His memoirs, entitled *The Vantage Point: Perspectives of the Presidency, 1963–1969,* were published in 1971.

Kennedy, John F. (1917–1963) 35th president of the United States, and the first Roman Catholic elected to the office. Before his election to the presidency, Kennedy served as a U.S. Senator and, during World War II, as the commander of a PT boat. He also wrote the Pulitzer-Prize-winning *Profiles in Courage* (1956), an account of some decisive moments in history when congressional leaders chose to act on their conscience rather than succumb to political pressure. As president, Kennedy oversaw the disastrous Bay of Pigs Invasion but emerged victorious over the Soviet Union in the Cuban Missile Crisis. Lee Harvey Oswald assassinated Kennedy on November 22, 1963.

Khrushchev, Nikita (1894–1971) Secretary of the Communist Party of the Soviet Union from 1953 to 1964, Khrushchev rose to power after the death of Stalin in 1953. He was the first Soviet official to speak out against Stalinism, a somewhat shocking move that became known as the "secret speech." Khrushchev was a firm believer in the Commmunist system and seemed earnestly to believe that communism would come to destroy democracy around the world. Following the Cuban Missile Crisis, he was deposed in 1964, partially because of his handling of the missle crisis.

Kinsey, Alfred C. (1894–1956) Trained primarily as a zoologist, Kinsey published two highly influential studies on human sexual behavior, together known as the Kinsey Reports. The first of these was *Sexual Behavior of the Human Male* (1948); the second was *Sexual Behavior of the Human Female* (1953). His frank treatment of human sexuality opened up new avenues of exploration in the realms of popular psychology and sociology. Although critics have since challenged several of Kinsey's claims, the reports are perhaps best remembered for their impact on American attitudes about sex.

King, Martin Luther (1929–1968) King was a civil rights leader who promoted a policy of nonviolent protest and passive resistance in the spirit of Indian leader Mohandas Gandhi. The boycott of the Montgomery, Alabama, bus system in 1955 is a good example of the kind of peaceful but powerful strategies King employed. The boycott was effective in that it led the Supreme Court to declare the segregation of

transportation unconstitutional. King is remembered as a remarkably talented orator. His most famous speech, "I Have a Dream," was delivered on the steps of the Lincoln Memorial in Washington, D.C. on August 28, 1963. A year later King was awarded the Nobel Peace Prize. In 1968 King was assassinated by petty thief James Earl Ray.

Lowell, Robert (1917–1977) One of the quintessential New England poets, Lowell was born in Boston, Massachusetts in 1917. Lowell is considered the founder and one of the master practitioners of the "confessional" school of American poetry, largely owing to his 1959 volume, *Life Studies*. In it, Lowell openly discusses his own troubled childhood. In his remaining years, Lowell continued to write important poems, most notably the title poem from *For the Union Dead* (1964), and became increasingly politically active. He befriended the Kennedy's and marched on the Pentagon in Washington, DC, with Norman Mailer, an account of which can be found in Mailer's *The Armies of the Night* (1968).

Mailer, Norman (b. 1923) One of the most influential novelists, journalists, and essayists of the post-World War II era, Mailer rose to national attention with his first novel, *The Naked and the Dead,* which was based on some of his own army experiences. It is considered one of the most important novels to come out of the War. In 1957, Mailer wrote an extremely controversial article entitled "The White Negro." Since then he has written on such topics as the Democratic Convention in 1968, the Vietnam War, and the execution of convicted murderer Gary Gilmore. Always interested in self-promotion, Mailer collected a number of his short stories and essays in a volume entitled *Advertisements for Myself*. His account of the 1967 peace march on the Pentagon is considered a landmark text in the field of literary journalism.

Malcolm X (1925–1965) Born Malcolm Little in 1925, X changed his name to protest the fact that the surnames of many African Americans were derived from the surnames of their masters. X was a vocal civil rights activist and member of the Nation of Islam. He rose through the ranks of Islam until he discovered that its leader, Elijah Muhammad, was in violation of several of its tenets. X broke with the group and founded the Muslim Mosque in 1964. In 1965, he was assassinated on stage by three gunmen affiliated with the Nation of Islam. X's "by any means necessary" approach to civil rights is often contrasted with Martin Luther King's passive resistance.

McCarthy, Joseph (1908–1957) A politician first elected to the U.S. Senate from the state of

Wisconsin in 1946. In 1950 McCarthy asserted that the U.S. State Department had been infiltrated by Communist agents. McCarthy gained national attention for this political move, though he was unable to back up any of his charges. McCarthy then proposed a series of Senate sub-committee hearings in which he continued to investigate the supposed presence of Communist sympathizers and Soviet spies in U.S. government and industry. McCarthy was eventually condemned by his fellow Senators for his false accusations. In the decades since the hearings, "McCarthyism" has come to denote the use of unconfirmed suspicions or rumors to play upon fears.

Momaday, N. Scott (b. 1934) In 1969, N. Scott Momaday became the first Native American to win the Pulitzer Prize. *House Made of Dawn,* his first novel, was an overwhelming critical and popular success. When he was growing up, both his parents worked as teachers on a nearby reservation. This gave him exposure not only to the Kiowa traditions of his father's family but many other Southwest Indian traditions. After publishing *House Made of Dawn,* Momaday moved to the University of California at Berkeley where he designed a graduate program of Indian Studies. A few years later, he published "The American Land Ethic" an essay intended to educate the American public as to the respect Indians held for the land. Momaday's memoir, *The Names,* appeared in 1976. His more recent novels include *The Ancient Child* (1989) and *In the Presence of the Sun* (1991).

Morrison, Toni (b. 1931) Winner of the 1993 Nobel Prize for Literature, Morrison is often considered the most significant African-American writer living today. Morrison published her first novel in 1970. Since then she has published nearly a dozen more including the most recent, *Love* (2003). Among Morrison's most widely read novels are *Beloved, Jazz, Sula, Song of Solomon,* and *The Bluest Eye*. She has also written a number of influential critical texts including *Playing in the Dark,* an examination of roles African Americans have traditionally played in Western canonical fiction. Upon awarding her the Prize, the Nobel Committee declared that her "novels invite the reader to partake at many levels, and at varying degrees of complexity. Still, the most enduring impression they leave is of empathy, compassion with one's fellow human beings."

Nixon, Richard M. (1913–1994) 37th President of the United States, Nixon also served as Vice President under Dwight D. Eisenhower. Nixon was a highly influential statesman, visiting Central and South America, the Soviet Union, and China during his Presidency. His trip to China in particular was hailed as a significant diplomatic move. Nixon also began the process of withdrawing troops from Vietnam and initiated a policy in which the United States would send foreign aid as opposed to troops in future conflicts. Nixon's foreign diplomacy and domestic policies will always be overshadowed by the Watergate scandal that led to his resignation from the Presidency in 1974. In 2005, the informant known only as "Deep Throat," who helped reporters Bob Woodward and Carl Bernstein uncover the scandal was revealed to be Mark Felt, then deputy director of the FBI.

Plath, Sylvia (1932–1963) Plath's life was one of tremendous creative highs and equally powerful personal chaos. Plath published her first poem at age eight, the same year her father died. Throughout her adolescence, she continued to write creatively and eventually entered Smith College. While at Smith, Plath attempted suicide, the events surrounding which she later reflected upon in an autobiographical novel called *The Bell Jar,* which was published in 1963. In 1956, Plath married the English poet, Ted Hughes, but became terribly depressed as a result. She killed herself in 1963 at the age of 30. *Ariel,* collection of her later poems, was published in 1965—the volume reveals Plath to have been at the height of her powers when she died.

Pynchon, Thomas (b. 1937) Not much is known about Pynchon's life outside of his brilliant works of fiction. He attended Cornell University where he studied Engineering Physics, until a two year stint in the Navy took him to the Mediterranean (the location for some of his first novel, *V.* [1963]). Pynchon returned to Cornell where he graduated in English, but then began a career at Boeing (the likely inspiration for the Yoyodyne Corporation in his second novel *The Crying of Lot 49* [1966]). Pynchon has continued to publish novels since the early sixties, most notably *Gravity's Rainbow* (1973) and *Mason & Dixon* (1997). Recently, Pynchon broke his many decades silence by appearing on an episode of the *Simpsons* called, "Diatribe of a Mad Housewife."

Rich, Adrienne (b. 1929) Poet, critic, and lecturer, Rich has exerted a tremendous influence on the landscape of contemporary poetry and is among the most popular poets writing today. An outspoken feminist, Rich's work tends to focus on issues of sexuality as well as women's social roles. Her two most significant collections of poems are *The Will to Change* and *Diving into the Wreck*. Perhaps her most important work of nonfiction is *Of*

Woman Born; in it, Rich rails against the strictures imposed by the fact of motherhood at the same time that she offers a moving presentation of the mothering process.

Salinger, J.D. (b. 1919) A highly influential and reclusive American author, whose most popular work *The Catcher in the Rye* came to define a generation of teenage disillusionment. Salinger participated in storming the beach at Normandy during World War II. This experience, along with a troubled relationship with his father, seem to have taken their toll on Salinger's personal life. Since the mid 1960s he has mostly kept to himself, apparently finding solace in the exploration of Eastern religions. It is rumored that he still continues to write, although he has published little since.

Tse-Tung, Mao (Zedong) (1893–1976) An influential politician and thinker, Mao controlled Communist China for over 25 years. A well-read and thoughtful person, Mao rose to power following a civil war with Chiang Kai-Shek and his Kuomintang, or nationalist party, and created the People's Republic of China in 1949. Mao's Communist aims differed from those of the Soviet Union and the two countries severed diplomatic ties following the "Great Leap Forward," Mao's attempt to revitalize the Chinese economy through agriculture as opposed to industry. Following the failure of the plan, Mao's leadership was threatened, and, in 1966, he declared a "cultural revolution," a bloody battle against intellectuals, traditional Chinese values, and the middle-class, which was carried out by Chinese youth.

Vonnegut, Kurt (b. 1922) A popular writer, critic, and literary personality, Vonnegut worked for General Electric before becoming a writer in 1950. Vonnegut's work often combines humor with an earnest concern for the state of humanity. His most famous novel, *Slaughterhouse-Five,* is a scathing denunciation of war. It is partially based on Vonnegut's own imprisonment in Dresden during the Allied fire bombings which killed as many as 135,000 people. Vonnegut also likes to incorporate themes from speculative science fiction into his novels.

Warhol, Andy (1928–1987) U.S. graphic artist, painter, and filmmaker, famous for the declaration that "everyone will be famous for 15 minutes." Warhol is most often associated with the Pop Art movement, which used images from ordinary household items like soup cans and dollar bills. He was involved in popularizing the art of silkscreening. Warhol explored ideas of repetition in his art and in film. Both his art and his films were mass-produced at his New York Studio, The Factory. His film *Chelsea Girls* (1966) is often cited as the first "art house" film to be shown to large audiences.

FURTHER READING

Chapter 1. American Literature Since 1945

Hassan, Ihab. *Contemporary American Literature: 1945–1972: An Introduction.* New York: Unger, 1972.

Kiernan, Robert F. *American Writing Since 1945: A Critical Survey.* New York: Unger, 1983.

Spiller, Robert, et al. *Literary History of the United States,* 4th edition. New York: Macmillan, 1974.

Chapter 2. The Fifties

Bellow, Saul. *Herzog.* New York: Penguin Classics, 2003.

Ellison, Ralph. *Invisible Man.* New York: Vintage, 1995.

Nabokov, Vladimir. *Lolita.* New York: Vintage, 1991.

O'Connor, Flannery. *Wise Blood.* New York: Farrar, Straus & Giroux, 1962.

Salinger, J.D. *The Catcher in the Rye.* New York: Little, Brown, 1991.

Chapter 3. The Sixties

Capote, Truman. *In Cold Blood.* New York: Vintage, 1994.

Kesey, Ken. *One Flew over the Cuckoo's Nest.* New York: Signet Book, 1989.

Mailer, Norman. *The Armies of the Night.* New York: Plume, 1995.

Morrison, Toni. *Song of Solomon.* New York: Plume, 1987.

Vonnegut, Kurt. *Cat's Cradle.* New York: Delta, 1998.

Updike, John. *Rabbit Run.* New York: Ballantine Books, 1999.

Chapter 4. Modern American Poetry

Espada, Martin. *Imagine the Angels of Bread.* New York: W. W. Norton, 1996.

Forché, Carolyn, ed. *Against Forgetting: Twenteth-Century Poetry of Witness.* New York: W. W. Norton, 1993.

Lowell, Robert. *Life Studies & For the Union Dead.* New York: Farrar, Straus & Giroux, 1967.

Nelson, Cary, ed. *Anthology of Modern American Poetry.* New York: Oxford University Press, 1999.

Plath, Sylvia. *Collected Poems.* New York: Perennial, 1981.

Rich, Adrienne. *The Fact of a Doorframe: Poems 1950–2001, New Edition.* New York: W. W. Norton, 2002.

Chapter 5. New Voices

Anzaldua, Gloria. *Borderlands/La Frontera: The New Mestiza.* San Francisco: Aunt Lute Books, 1999.

Cisneros, Sandra. *The House on Mango Street.* New York: Knopf, 1994.

Kingston, Maxine Hong. *China Men.* New York: Vintage, 1989.

Lahiri, Jhumpa. *Interpreter of Maladies.* Boston: Mariner Books, 1999.

Momaday, N. Scott. *House Made of Dawn.* New York: Perennial Classics, 1999.

Palumbo-Lu, David, ed. *The Ethnic Canon.* Minneapolis: University of Minnesota Press, 1995.

Tan, Amy. *The Joy Luck Club.* New York: Ivy Books, 1990.

Chapter 6. The Postmodern Moment

Carver, Raymond. *What We Talk about When We Talk about Love.* New York: Vintage, 1989.

DeLillo, Don. *White Noise.* New York: Penguin Books, 1991.

Kuhn, Thomas. *The Structure of Scientific Revolutions.* Chicago: The University of Chicago Press, 1996.

McCarthy, Cormac. *Blood Meridian: Or the Evening Redness in the West.* New York: Vintage, 1992.

Pynchon, Thomas. *The Crying of Lot 49.* New York: Perennial, 1999.

INDEX

DATE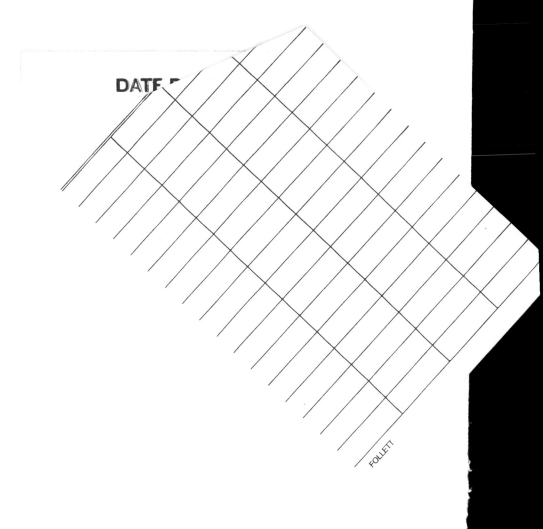

FOLLETT